ASHFAAQ A. KHAN

AI and The Art of Business: A Guide to Creative Entrepreneurship

BlueRose ONE.com DIY
Stories Matter
NewDelhi • London

BLUEROSE PUBLISHERS
India | U.K.

BlueRose ONE.com DIY
Stories Matter
NewDelhi • London

For permissions requests or inquiries regarding this publication, please contact:

BLUEROSE PUBLISHERS
www.BlueRoseONE.com
info@bluerosepublishers.com
+91 8882 898 898
+4407342408967

ISBN: 978-93-7542-946-3

First Edition: January 2026

DEDICATION

To my Family and (would be) Entrepreneurs.

To the dreamers who dare to question,
the thinkers who crave clarity,
and the quiet hearts that carry untold stories.
This book, "AI and The Art of Business: A Guide to Creative Entrepreneurship," is for you—
for every beginning that needed courage,
every boundary that demanded crossing,
and every chapter of life that taught us
the power of becoming.
May these pages find you at the right moment.

IN today's competitive market, creativity and innovation are key to success. AI and The Art of Business: A Guide to Creative Entrepreneurship explores how creativity drives entrepreneurship, offering practical advice, real-world examples, and inspiring stories from successful entrepreneurs. This Book highlights the importance of creative thinking in solving problems and fuelling business growth, while providing actionable strategies to help readers develop and apply their own ideas.

— The AUTHOR

Contents

Preface

THIS millennium and the 21st century belong to creative entrepreneurs who possess their own critical thought processes. In the years and decades ahead, I hope that Gen Z, along with their peers and patrons, will fully capitalise on the opportunities available to them.

I believe that 'An idea can change your life.' Therefore, I understand that there is definitely something for every aspiring entrepreneur who can read between the lines in this book. To me, reading between the lines means looking for or discovering a meaning that is implied rather than explicitly stated. Our thought processes are too complex to fully comprehend, and each of us has a unique thought process and mindset of our own.

In the ever-evolving landscape of business, where new ideas emerge and industries are disrupted, entrepreneurship has become a driving force of innovation and progress. ***AI and The Art of Business: A Guide to Creative Entrepreneurship*** is not just about profits and numbers; it is a testament to the human spirit, ingenuity, and the relentless pursuit of turning dreams into reality.

This work is an invaluable compendium of useful information on creative entrepreneurship based on my professional journey. It encompasses pitfalls, successes, glory, and failures — indeed, a tryst with my career over the past two decades despite having low vision. My journey as an entrepreneur, and my pursuit of what I always desired, are well-documented in an easy-to-read format. I have approached this path with optimism rather than the despair that often leads many on their quest for success into depression.

AI and The Art of Business: A Guide to Creative Entrepreneurship is a culmination of wisdom, insights, and practical advice crafted to empower aspiring entrepreneurs and seasoned business leaders alike. This guidebook is an exploration into the realms of creativity and entrepreneurship, illuminating the paths to success and providing tools to navigate the challenges that lie ahead.

I must tell you that writing a book is quite tough. Considering the different phases of writing is like putting everything together, stitched in size and order. The content for this book began with jotting down ideas at 20:47 IST on 7th May 2023. Thereafter, for a few months, I could hardly write or edit due to my health. I finished the AI portion in January 2024 and gave the work its final touches for publishing. I added another chapter that summer. This is my debut book, and I look forward to sharing more with you soon. Discover my work at https://ashfaaq.com.

In a world where traditional notions of business are being challenged, creativity has emerged as a powerful catalyst for growth and differentiation. The convergence of technology, globalisation, and changing consumer needs demands an entrepreneurial mindset that embraces innovation, adaptability, and unconventional thinking. It is this fusion of creativity and entrepreneurship that forms the foundation of this book.

Drawing inspiration from the stories of visionary entrepreneurs and industry pioneers, ***AI and The Art of Business: A Guide to Creative***

Entrepreneurship invites you on a journey to explore the multifaceted nature of entrepreneurship. It delves into the mindset required to spot opportunities in unexpected places, to take calculated risks, and to relentlessly pursue excellence in all endeavours. Through the pages of this book, you will discover the importance of cultivating a creative mindset, building a strong foundation for your business, nurturing relationships, and fostering resilience in the face of adversity.

AI and The Art of Business: A Guide to Creative Entrepreneurship is not a prescriptive manual with a one-size-fits-all formula for success. Instead, it serves as a guide that offers principles, strategies, and frameworks to help you forge your own path as a creative entrepreneur. It encourages you to embrace your uniqueness, to think outside the box, and to challenge the status quo. It recognises that creativity is not limited to the realm of artists and designers but permeates every aspect of business, from marketing and branding to product development and customer experience.

As you embark on your entrepreneurial journey, let this book be your trusted companion — a source of inspiration, guidance, and encouragement. It is not meant to provide all the answers but rather to spark new questions, to ignite your imagination, and to empower you to create a business that not only thrives but also makes a lasting impact.

Remember, entrepreneurship is an art — a canvas upon which you can paint your dreams, a symphony you compose with passion and purpose. ***AI and The Art of Business: A Guide to Creative Entrepreneurship*** invites you to harness your creativity, seize the opportunities that surround you, and embark on a transformative journey that will redefine the way you approach business.

Business can never be taught; it is an experience unique to everyone. The success of a business depends on numerous factors and conditions specific to each individual. One can certainly learn from others' mistakes and experiences, but no one can simply copy or replicate another person's success. Success for an entrepreneur is also unique to each individual. While the concept of business is universal, the methods and strategies to develop and nurture it vary across domains and regions.

May this book empower you to unlock your full potential, to unleash your creative spirit, and to embark on a path of entrepreneurial success that transcends boundaries and redefines what is possible.

Let the art of business begin!

ASHFAAQ A. Khan | **https://ashfaaq.com** | IN | 14 July 2024

Disclaimer

THE Author and Publisher of this (e)Book have used their best efforts in preparing this (e)Book. The information contained in this (e)Book is strictly for motivation, information and educational purposes. The Author makes no representation or warranties with respect to the accuracy, applicability, fitness, or completeness of the contents of this (e)Book. It is sold online and offline with the understanding that the Author is not engaged to render any type of psychological, legal, or any other kind of professional advice. The content of each chapter is the sole expression and opinion of the Author. No warranties or guarantees are expressed or implied by the Author's choice to include any of the content in this (e)Book. The Author shall not be liable for any physical, psychological, emotional, financial, or commercial damages, including, but not limited to, special, incidental, consequential or other damages. Author's views and rights are the same: You are responsible for your own choices, actions, and results. Therefore, if you wish to apply ideas contained in this (e)Book, you are taking full responsibility for your actions.

Acknowledgments

Words cannot express my gratitude. Everyone offers encouragement when you're successful, but I am especially thankful to those who discouraged me.

Prologue

"20 years of experience condensed into fewer than 200 pages"

IN the dynamic realm of entrepreneurship, where creativity and commerce converge, ***AI and The Art of Business: A Guide to Creative Entrepreneurship*** unfolds as a beacon for visionaries and trailblazers. This prologue invites you to embark on a transformative journey, navigating the intricate tapestry of innovation and enterprise.

In the crucible of this narrative, we explore the fusion of artistry and strategy, unlocking the secrets to sculpting a thriving venture with the finesse of a master craftsman. As we traverse the landscapes of inspiration and practicality, we delve into the stories of those who dared to dream differently, drawing invaluable lessons from the alchemy of their successes and failures.

This guide is not just a manual but a living testament to the notion that entrepreneurship is an art form, a canvas upon which dreams are painted with the vibrant hues of ambition and ingenuity. It challenges conventional thinking, urging readers to embrace uncertainty as a crucible for innovation and to sculpt their business endeavours with an artist's mindset.

As we embark on this odyssey, let the pages of ***AI and The Art of Business: A Guide to Creative Entrepreneurship*** serve as a compass, navigating the uncharted waters of creative entrepreneurship, and illuminating the path towards a future where commerce transcends mere transaction, evolving into a masterpiece of strategic brilliance and imaginative daring.

Introduction

Definition of Creative Entrepreneurship

CREATIVE entrepreneurship is a term that has gained immense popularity in recent times. It refers to a new breed of entrepreneurs who are driven by passion, creativity, and innovation. They bring a unique perspective to the business world, one that is rooted in the arts and creative expression. Creative entrepreneurship is not just about starting a business; it's about creating something that is truly unique and meaningful.

At its core, creative entrepreneurship is all about combining the artistic and the commercial. It's about taking an idea or a concept and turning it into a successful business venture. This requires a unique set of skills that go beyond traditional business acumen. Creative entrepreneurs need to be able to think outside the box, take risks, and be willing to experiment with new ideas.

One of the most defining characteristics of creative entrepreneurship is the emphasis on originality and innovation. Creative entrepreneurs are not content with simply following the trends; they want to create something that is truly new and groundbreaking. This requires a deep understanding of the market, as well as the ability to identify gaps and opportunities that others have overlooked.

Another important aspect of creative entrepreneurship is the focus on collaboration and community. Creative entrepreneurs understand that they cannot succeed alone – they need to build strong networks and partnerships in order to achieve their goals. This requires a willingness to share ideas and resources, and to work collaboratively with others in the industry.

Ultimately, creative entrepreneurship is about creating value – both for the entrepreneur and for society as a whole. It's about using creativity and innovation to solve problems, create new products and services, and improve people's lives. This requires a deep commitment to the creative process, as well as a willingness to take risks and push the boundaries of what is possible.

In conclusion, creative entrepreneurship is a dynamic and exciting field that offers endless opportunities for those with a passion for innovation and creativity. By combining artistic vision with business acumen, creative entrepreneurs can create truly unique and meaningful ventures that have the potential to change the world.

Importance of Creative Entrepreneurship

CREATIVE entrepreneurship is an essential aspect of business that can help entrepreneurs to stand out from the crowd. It is the art of combining creativity with entrepreneurship to create innovative, unique, and sustainable businesses. Creative entrepreneurship is not just about creating new products and services; it is also about creating new ways of doing business. In this sub chapter, we will discuss the importance of creative entrepreneurship for entrepreneurs and the niches of creative entrepreneurship.

One of the most significant benefits of creative entrepreneurship is its ability to help entrepreneurs differentiate their businesses from their competitors. Creative entrepreneurs are always looking for new and innovative ways to do things. They are not satisfied with the status quo and are always pushing the boundaries of what is possible. This mindset allows them to create products, services, and business models that are truly unique and stand out from the crowd.

Another benefit of creative entrepreneurship is its ability to foster innovation. Creative entrepreneurs are always looking for new and better ways to do things. They are not afraid to take risks and try new things. This mindset leads to the development of new products, services, and business models that can disrupt entire industries. Creative entrepreneurs are often the ones responsible for creating new markets and driving economic growth.

Creative entrepreneurship is also essential for the niches of creative entrepreneurship. These niches include industries such as fashion, design, music, art, and film. Creative entrepreneurs in these industries are responsible for creating new trends, styles, and cultural movements. They are the ones who shape the culture and influence the way we think, act, and consume.

Finally, creative entrepreneurship is crucial for entrepreneurs who want to make a positive impact on the world. Creative entrepreneurs are often driven by a desire to change the world for the better. They are not just focused on making money; they are also focused on creating a better world for future generations. This mindset leads to the development of businesses that are socially and environmentally responsible, and that contribute to the greater good.

In conclusion, creative entrepreneurship is an essential aspect of business that can help entrepreneurs to stand out from the crowd, foster innovation, create new markets, shape culture, and make a positive impact on the world. As an entrepreneur in the niches of creative entrepreneurship, it is important to embrace creativity and innovation, take risks, and create businesses that are truly unique and socially responsible.

Overview of the Book

AI and The Art of Business: A Guide to Creative Entrepreneurship is a comprehensive guidebook for entrepreneurs seeking inspiration and guidance in their creative endeavours. This book is aimed at entrepreneurs who are looking to build a business in the creative industry or incorporate creative elements into their existing business.

This book is divided into three main sections. The first section focuses on the basics of entrepreneurship, including defining your target market, creating a business plan, and developing a marketing strategy. The second section delves into the world of creative entrepreneurship, discussing the importance of creativity in business and exploring the various creative industries, including art, design, fashion, music, and film. The third section focuses on the practical aspects of running a creative business, including managing finances, building a team, and scaling your business with the use of Artificial Intelligence (AI).

AI and The Art of Business: A Guide to Creative Entrepreneurship is a testament to entrepreneurs who have successfully built businesses in their respective industries. As the author, I share their decisions, actions, and insights, offering readers with a behind-the-scenes look at what it takes to succeed as a creative entrepreneur.

This book is filled with practical advice, tips, and tools that entrepreneurs can use to build and grow their businesses.

One of the key themes of the book is the importance of creativity in business. The entrepreneurs featured affirm that creativity is not just a nice-to-have, but a fundamental ingredient for success in the modern business world. This book provides numerous examples of successful businesses that have leveraged creativity to stand out from the competition and build a loyal customer base.

AI and The Art of Business: A Guide to Creative Entrepreneurship is a must-read for entrepreneurs looking to build a business in the creative industry or incorporate creative elements into their existing business. This book provides readers with a comprehensive overview of the key concepts, strategies, and tools needed to succeed as a creative entrepreneur. Whether you are just starting out or looking to take your business to the next level, this book is an invaluable resource for anyone looking to succeed in the world of creative entrepreneurship.

THE MINDSET OF A CREATIVE ENTREPRENEUR

Characteristics of a Creative Entrepreneur

THE success of any entrepreneurial venture depends on the creativity and innovation of the entrepreneur. In order to excel in the field of creative entrepreneurship, it is essential to possess certain characteristics which set apart the successful entrepreneurs from the rest.

Here are some of the key characteristics that define a successful creative entrepreneur:

- **Passion and Drive**: A creative entrepreneur is passionate about their work and has a drive to succeed. They are highly motivated and focused on achieving their goals, no matter what obstacles come their way.
- **Vision and Creativity**: Creativity is the cornerstone of a successful creative entrepreneur. They have a unique vision and are able to think outside the box, coming up with innovative solutions to problems.
- **Risk Tolerance**: Creative entrepreneurs are not afraid to take risks.

They understand that failure is a part of the learning process and are willing to take calculated risks in order to achieve their goals.

- **Flexibility and Adaptability**: A creative entrepreneur is flexible and adaptable, able to pivot their business model as needed. They are open to feedback and willing to make changes in order to improve and grow their business.
- **Resilience**: Creative entrepreneurs are resilient and able to bounce back from setbacks and failures. They understand that success is not always linear and are able to persevere through difficult times.
- **Networking and Collaboration**: A successful creative entrepreneur understands the importance of networking and collaboration. They are able to build relationships with others in their industry and work collaboratively to achieve common goals.

The characteristics of a successful creative entrepreneur are a unique blend of passion, vision, creativity, risk tolerance, flexibility, resilience, and networking and collaboration. By cultivating these traits, entrepreneurs can position themselves for success in the exciting and dynamic world of creative entrepreneurship.

Developing a Growth Mindset

ONE of the most important aspects of being a successful entrepreneur is having a growth mindset. This means having an attitude of openness and a willingness to learn and grow in order to achieve your goals. A growth mindset is essential for creative entrepreneurship because in this field, innovation and adaptation are key to success.

To develop a growth mindset, it is important to start by recognising that your abilities and talents are not fixed, but can be developed and improved upon through effort and learning. This means embracing challenges and seeing them as opportunities to learn and grow, rather than as obstacles to be avoided.

Another important aspect of developing a growth mindset is a willingness to take risks and try new things. Creative entrepreneurship is all about innovation and pushing boundaries, and this requires a willingness to step out of your comfort zone and take calculated risks.

It is also important to surround yourself with people who have a growth mindset. This means seeking out mentors and peers who are supportive, encouraging, and open to new ideas. It also means being willing to learn from feedback and criticism, and using it as an opportunity to improve and grow.

Finally, it is important to cultivate a sense of resilience and perseverance. Creative entrepreneurship can be a challenging and unpredictable journey, and setbacks and failures are inevitable. However, with a growth mindset, you can see these challenges as opportunities to learn and grow, and to ultimately achieve your goals.

In summary, developing a growth mindset is essential for success in creative entrepreneurship. By embracing challenges, taking risks, surrounding yourself with supportive people, and cultivating resilience, you can develop the mindset needed to achieve your goals and thrive in this exciting and dynamic field.

Importance of Failure

AS entrepreneurs, we often focus on success and forget about the importance of failure. The truth is that failure is an essential part of the entrepreneurial journey, and we should embrace it rather than fear it. In this chapter, we will explore why failure is crucial for creative entrepreneurship.

Firstly, failure helps us learn and grow. When we fail, we gain valuable insights into what went wrong and how we can improve. These insights are crucial for future success. Without failure, we would not have the opportunity to learn from our mistakes and make the necessary adjustments to our business.

Secondly, failure builds resilience. As entrepreneurs, we face numerous challenges and setbacks. Failure teaches us how to bounce back and keep going despite the obstacles. It helps us develop the mental toughness needed to overcome adversity. The ability to persevere in the face of failure is a critical trait for creative entrepreneurship.

Thirdly, failure fosters creativity. When we fail, we are forced to think outside the box and come up with new solutions to our problems. This process of creative problem-solving can lead to innovation and breakthroughs that we may not have discovered otherwise. Failure can be a catalyst for creativity and can help us find new and better ways of doing things.

Lastly, failure helps us build a growth mindset. A growth mindset is the belief that our abilities and intelligence can be developed through hard work and dedication. When we fail, we are forced to confront our weaknesses and work on improving them. This process of growth and self-improvement is essential for creative entrepreneurship.

In conclusion, failure is not something to be feared but rather embraced. It is an essential part of the entrepreneurial journey and teaches us valuable lessons about learning, resilience, creativity, and growth. As entrepreneurs, we should view failure as an opportunity for growth and use it to our advantage.

FINDING YOUR PASSION

Identifying Your Passion

CREATIVE entrepreneurship is all about pursuing your passion and turning it into a successful business venture. However, before you can turn your passion into a profitable business, you need to first identify what your passion is. In this sub-chapter, we will explore some strategies and techniques that can help you identify your passion.

1. **Reflect on your interests and hobbies**: Start by taking some time to reflect on your interests and hobbies. What activities do you enjoy doing in your free time? What topics do you enjoy reading about or learning about? Identify the things that make you feel energised and engaged.
2. **Consider your values and beliefs**: Your passion is often linked to your values and beliefs. Consider what issues or causes you feel strongly about. What do you believe in and stand for? Identifying your values and beliefs can help you to find a passion that aligns with your principles.
3. **Look for patterns**: Another way to identify your passion is to look for patterns in your life. What activities have you consistently

enjoyed throughout your life? What experiences have been the most meaningful or impactful? Identifying patterns can help you to identify a passion that you may have overlooked.

4. **Try new things**: Sometimes, your passion may be something that you have not yet discovered. Trying new things can help you to identify new interests and passions. Take a class, attend a workshop, or try a new hobby to explore new opportunities and discover what truly excites you.
5. **Ask for feedback**: Finally, don't be afraid to ask for feedback from others. Talk to friends, family members, and colleagues about your interests and passions. They may be able to provide valuable insights and perspectives that can help you to identify your true passion.

Once you have identified your passion, you can begin to explore ways to turn it into a successful business venture. Remember, pursuing your passion is not always easy, but it can be incredibly rewarding. Stay true to yourself and your values, and you will be well on your way to achieving creative entrepreneurship success.

Turning Your Passion into a Business Idea

WHEN it comes to starting a business, one of the most important factors to consider is your passion. Passion is the driving force that fuels your creativity, motivation, and determination. If you're passionate about something, you're more likely to put in the hard work and long hours required to succeed.

To turn your passion into a business idea, you need to start by identifying what it is that you love to do. This could be anything from baking cupcakes to designing websites to writing poetry. Once you've identified your passion, you need to start thinking about how you can turn it into a viable business.

The first step is to do some research. Look at what other businesses are doing in your industry and see how you can differentiate yourself. Identify your target market and figure out what they're looking for in a product or service like yours. This will help you to develop a unique value proposition that sets you apart from the competition.

Next, you need to start developing your business plan. This should include everything from your marketing strategy to your financial projections. Be sure to include a detailed description of your product or service, your target market, and your competitive advantage. This will help you to stay focused and on track as you start to build your business.

Once you have your business plan in place, it's time to start putting it into action. This could mean setting up a website, creating a social media presence, or networking with other entrepreneurs in your industry. Whatever you do, make sure that you're staying true to your passion and your values.

Starting a business is never easy, but if you're passionate about what you're doing, it can be one of the most rewarding experiences of your life. By turning your passion into a business idea, you're giving yourself the opportunity to do something you love every day while also building a successful and profitable company. Remember to stay focused, stay motivated, and stay true to your values, and you'll be well on your way to success.

Researching Your Business Idea

AS a creative entrepreneur, it's easy to get caught up in the excitement of a new business idea. However, before diving in head first, it's important to thoroughly research and validate your concept. This will not only help you understand the viability of your idea, but it will also help you identify potential roadblocks and opportunities for growth.

Here are some tips for researching your business idea:

1. **Identify your target market**: Who is your ideal customer? What are their needs and pain points? Conduct market research to gather data on your target audience's demographics, behaviour, and preferences.

2. **Analyse the competition**: Who are your competitors? What are their strengths and weaknesses? What sets your business apart from theirs? Conduct a competitive analysis to gain a better understanding of the market landscape.

3. **Test your idea**: Before investing time and money into your business, test your idea with a focus group or survey. This will help you gauge interest and gather feedback to refine your concept.

4. **Create a business plan**: A well-thought-out business plan is essential for any entrepreneur. It should include a detailed description of your business, target market, competition, marketing and sales strategies, financial projections, and more.

5. **Seek feedback**: Don't be afraid to seek feedback from trusted advisors, mentors, or even potential customers. This can help you identify blind

spots and ensure that your business idea is on the right track.

Remember, researching your business idea is an ongoing process. As you launch and grow your business, continue to gather feedback, analyse data, and make adjustments as needed. By doing so, you'll increase your chances of success in the competitive world of creative entrepreneurship.

CREATING A BUSINESS PLAN

Importance of a Business Plan

AS an entrepreneur, it can be easy to get caught up in the excitement of starting a business without taking the time to create a formal business plan. However, this can be a critical mistake that could ultimately lead to failure. A business plan is an essential tool that every entrepreneur should have in their arsenal. It provides a roadmap for your business and outlines your goals, strategies, and financial projections.

One of the most significant benefits of having a business plan is that it forces you to think critically about your business idea. It requires you to research and analyse your target market, competition, and industry trends. This information can help you identify potential challenges and opportunities and develop strategies to overcome them. It also helps you identify your unique value proposition and define your brand, which is essential in a competitive marketplace.

A business plan also serves as a communication tool. It allows you to articulate your vision, objectives, and strategies to potential investors, partners, and employees. Without a formal plan, it can be challenging to get others on board with your vision and secure the necessary funding to launch and grow your business.

Another critical benefit of a business plan is that it helps you stay on track and measure your progress. It provides a framework for setting and achieving goals and tracking your financial performance. This information is crucial for making informed decisions and adjusting your strategies as necessary.

In the world of creative entrepreneurship, a business plan is especially important. Creative businesses often face unique challenges, such as protecting intellectual property and managing cash flow. A formal plan can help you address these challenges and develop strategies that allow you to focus on your creative work while still running a profitable business.

In conclusion, a business plan is an essential tool for any entrepreneur, especially those in the creative industries. It provides a roadmap for your business, helps you identify potential challenges and opportunities, and serves as a communication tool for stakeholders. Without a formal plan, it can be challenging to get your business off the ground and achieve long-term success. So take the time to create a comprehensive plan that outlines your vision, goals, and strategies, and use it as a guide to navigate the challenges and opportunities of entrepreneurship.

Elements of a Business Plan

When starting a business, it's essential to have a well-crafted plan that outlines your goals, strategies, and resources. A business plan serves as a road map to guide your entrepreneurial journey and helps you make informed decisions along the way. In this sub chapter, we'll explore the key elements of a business plan that every creative entrepreneur should include.

1. **Executive Summary**: The executive summary is a brief overview of your business plan that provides an introduction to your business idea, product or service, target market, competition, financial projections, and goals. This section should be compelling and concise to capture the attention of potential investors or partners.
2. **Company Description**: In this section, you'll provide a detailed description of your business, including its name, legal structure, mission statement, and the problem your business solves. You'll also describe how your business will differentiate itself from competitors in the market.
3. **Market Analysis**: A market analysis is crucial for any business plan to identify the target market and competition. This section should include a thorough analysis of industry trends, target market demographics, market size, and competition. You'll also need to outline your marketing and sales strategies and how you plan to reach your target audience.
4. **Product or Service Line**: In this section, you'll describe your product or service in detail, including its features, benefits, and how it solves your target market's pain points. You'll also discuss your product's lifecycle and pricing strategy.
5. **Operations and Management**: This section outlines how your business will operate and who will be responsible for managing it. You'll discuss your business's day-to-day operations, including manufacturing, distribution, and customer service. You'll also introduce your management team and their roles and responsibilities.
6. **Financials**: The financial section of your business plan is critical

for attracting investors or securing funding. You'll need to provide financial projections, including cash flow, income statements, and balance sheets, for the next three to five years. You'll also need to discuss your funding needs and how you plan to repay investors or lenders.

Conclusion: In conclusion, creating a business plan is a crucial step in launching a successful creative entrepreneurship venture. The elements above are essential to include in your plan to ensure that you have a comprehensive and well-thought-out strategy to guide your business. Remember that a business plan is a living document that should be updated regularly to reflect changes in your business and the market.

Writing an Effective Business Plan

AS a creative entrepreneur, having an effective business plan is crucial to your success. A business plan is a road map that outlines your goals, strategies, and tactics for your business. It helps you stay focused and on track, and it also serves as a tool to attract investors and partners.

Here are some tips for writing an effective business plan:

1. **Define your mission and vision statement**: Your mission statement should define your business's purpose, while your vision statement should describe what you hope to achieve in the future. These statements should be clear and concise, and they should align with your brand values and goals.
2. **Conduct market research**: Your business plan should include a thorough analysis of your target market, competitors, and industry trends. This research will help you identify opportunities and

challenges in your market, and it will also help you develop strategies to overcome these challenges.

3. **Develop a marketing and sales strategy**: Your marketing and sales strategy should outline how you plan to promote and sell your products or services. This strategy should include your target audience, pricing strategy, distribution channels, and promotional tactics.
4. **Create a financial plan**: Your financial plan should include projected revenue and expenses, cash flow projections, and a break-even analysis. This plan will help you determine how much funding you need to start and grow your business, and it will also help you identify potential funding sources.
5. **Develop an operations plan**: Your operations plan should outline how you plan to manage your business on a day-to-day basis. This plan should include your staffing strategy, production processes, and supply chain management.
6. **Review and revise**: Once you have completed your business plan, it's important to review and revise it regularly.

Your business plan should be a living document that you can update as your business evolves.

In conclusion, writing an effective business plan is essential to the success of your creative entrepreneurship venture. By following these tips, you can develop a plan that will guide your business towards success.

FUNDING YOUR BUSINESS

Options for Financing Your Business

AS an entrepreneur, one of the most important aspects of starting and growing your own business is financing. Without money, it's impossible to bring your creative ideas to life. Fortunately, there are several options available to you for financing your business.

The first and most common option is to secure a loan from a bank or other financial institution. This can be a great option if you have a solid business plan and credit history. With a loan, you'll receive a lump sum of money that you can use to invest in your business. However, keep in mind that you'll be responsible for paying back the loan plus interest, so it's important to make sure you have a clear plan for how you'll use the money and how you'll generate revenue to pay it back.

Another option for financing your business is to seek out investors. This can be a great option if you have a unique business idea or a strong track record of success. Investors can provide you with the funds you need to get your business off the ground, and in exchange, they'll receive a share of the profits or equity in your company. Keep in mind that working with investors can be a complex process, and you'll need to be prepared to give up some control over your business.

Crowdfunding is another option for financing your business. This involves raising money through a large number of small contributions from a community of people who are interested in your business idea. Crowdfunding can be a great option if you have a strong online presence and a compelling story that resonates with potential donors. However, keep in mind that crowdfunding can be a time-consuming process, and you'll need to be prepared to put in the effort to promote your campaign and engage with your supporters.

Finally, you may be able to finance your business through grants or other forms of funding from government agencies or non-profit organisations. This can be a great option if you're working on a project that aligns with the goals of these organisations. However, keep in mind that the application process for grants can be competitive and time-consuming.

Ultimately, the key to financing your business is to understand your options and choose the one that best fits your needs and goals. With the right approach, you can secure the funding you need to bring your creative ideas to life and build a successful business.

Creating a Financial Plan

CREATING a financial plan is one of the most important steps in starting and growing a successful business. As a creative entrepreneur, you may have a lot of ideas and enthusiasm, but without a solid financial plan, your business may not survive for long.

The first step in creating a financial plan is to identify your business goals. What do you want to achieve? How much money do you need to make? What are your expenses? Understanding your goals and expenses will help you make informed financial decisions that will help you achieve your business goals.

The next step is to create a budget. Your budget should include all of your expenses, including rent, utilities, insurance, taxes, and salaries. You should also include any expenses associated with marketing and advertising, as well as any other costs associated with running your business.

Once you have created your budget, it is important to track your expenses regularly. This will help you identify any areas where you are overspending and make adjustments as necessary. You should also regularly review your budget to ensure that you are on track to meet your business goals.

Another important aspect of creating a financial plan is to establish a cash flow projection. A cash flow projection will help you understand when money is coming in and going out of your business. This will help you plan for any potential cash flow shortages and make adjustments as necessary.

In addition to creating a financial plan, it is important to regularly review and update your plan as your business grows and evolves. Your financial plan should be a living document that is updated regularly to reflect changes in your business and the market.

In conclusion, creating a financial plan is an essential step in starting and growing a successful business. By understanding your goals and expenses, creating a budget, tracking your expenses, establishing a cash flow projection, and regularly reviewing and updating your plan, you can make informed financial decisions that will help you achieve your business goals.

Pitching to Investors

ONE of the most important aspects of entrepreneurship is securing funding. Whether you're launching a new business or expanding an existing one, you need money to make it happen. And while there are many ways to raise capital, pitching to investors is often the most effective. In this subchapter, we'll discuss how to prepare for and deliver a successful pitch to investors.

Preparing for the Pitch

Before you even start to think about pitching to investors, you need to have a clear understanding of your business and its potential for growth. This means conducting thorough market research, understanding your competition, and developing a solid business plan that outlines your goals and how you plan to achieve them. You also need to have a team in place that has the skills and experience necessary to execute your plan.

Once you have done your homework, it's time to start preparing for the pitch. This involves putting together a compelling presentation that highlights the key aspects of your business, including your market opportunity, your unique value proposition, and your financial projections. You should also be prepared to answer tough questions from potential investors, so make sure you have a deep understanding of your business and can speak confidently about its strengths and weaknesses.

Delivering the Pitch

When it comes time to deliver your pitch, you want to make sure you're presenting yourself and your business in the best possible light. This means dressing professionally, speaking clearly and confidently, and maintaining eye contact with your audience. You should also be prepared to adjust your presentation on the fly based on the feedback you receive from investors.

During the pitch, you'll want to focus on the most important aspects of your business, including your market opportunity, your unique value proposition, and your financial projections. Make sure you're highlighting the areas that are most likely to capture the interest of your audience, and don't be afraid to use visual aids like slides and videos to help illustrate your points.

Closing the Deal

If all goes well, you'll be able to close the deal and secure funding for your business. To do this, you need to be prepared to negotiate the terms of the investment, including the amount of money you'll receive, the equity stake you'll give up, and any other conditions that may be attached to the investment. Make sure you have a clear understanding of what you're agreeing to, and don't be afraid to ask for advice from a lawyer or other trusted advisor.

In conclusion, pitching to investors is a critical part of the entrepreneurial process, and it's important to approach it with a clear understanding of your business and a well-prepared presentation. By following these tips, you can increase your chances of securing the funding you need to take your business to the next level.

BUILDING YOUR TEAM

Hiring the Right People

HIRING the right people is one of the most critical factors in the success of any business, especially in the field of creative entrepreneurship. Finding the right individuals who can bring creativity, innovation, and passion to your team can be challenging, but it is crucial to the growth and sustainability of your business.

Here are some tips to help you hire the right people for your creative business:

Define the Job Role

Before you start hiring, it is essential to define the job role and responsibilities clearly. You need to know what skills, experience, and qualifications the ideal candidate should have. This will help you attract the right candidates and ensure that they have the necessary skills and experience to perform the job successfully.

Look for Passion and Creativity

Creative entrepreneurs need people who are passionate about their work and have a creative mindset. Look for candidates who have a portfolio or samples of their work that showcase their creativity and skills. You want people who can bring fresh ideas and perspectives to your team and help you stand out from the competition.

Conduct Thorough Interviews

Interviews are a crucial part of the hiring process, and it is essential to conduct them thoroughly. Ask open-ended questions that encourage candidates to share their experiences and insights. This will help you gauge their skills, experience, and personality traits that are essential for the job.

Check References

Checking references is a critical step in the hiring process. It will help you verify the candidate's skills, experience, and work ethic. Contact their previous employers or colleagues to get a better understanding of their work style, strengths, and weaknesses.

Offer Competitive Compensation

Offering competitive compensation is crucial to attract and retain top talent. Research the market rates for similar job roles and offer a salary and benefits package that is competitive.

In conclusion, hiring the right people is essential for the success of any business, especially in creative entrepreneurship. By defining the job role, looking for passion and creativity, conducting thorough interviews, checking references, and offering competitive compensation, you can attract and retain top talent that will help your business thrive.

Creating a Company Culture

AS an entrepreneur, you are not just building a business, but also a company culture. This culture is the personality of your organisation and sets the tone for how your employees interact with each other and your customers.

Creating a company culture starts with defining your values, mission, and vision. These should be the guiding principles for everything your company does, from hiring to decision-making. Your values should reflect what is important to you as an entrepreneur and what you want your company to stand for. Your mission should be a clear statement of what your company does and why it exists. Your vision should be a picture of where you want your company to be in the future.

Once you have defined your values, mission, and vision, you need to communicate them clearly to your team. Make sure everyone understands what your company stands for and what you are trying to achieve. Encourage your team to embrace your values and help you achieve your mission and vision.

To create a strong company culture, you need to lead by example. If you want your team to be collaborative, then you need to be collaborative. If you want your team to be innovative, then you need to be innovative. Your behaviour sets the tone for your team, so make sure you are modelling the modelling you want to see.

Another important aspect of creating a company culture is hiring the right people. Look for candidates who share your values and are aligned with your mission and vision. Hire for culture fit, not just skills. You can always teach skills, but you can't teach someone to be a good fit for your company culture.

Finally, celebrate your successes and your failures. When you achieve a goal, celebrate it with your team. When you make a mistake, acknowledge it and learn from it. By doing this, you are creating a culture of learning and growth.

In summary, creating a company culture is about defining your values, mission, and vision, communicating them clearly to your team, leading by example, hiring the right people, and celebrating your successes and failures. By doing this, you can build a strong company culture that will help you achieve your goals and make your business a success.

Managing Your Team Effectively

AS an entrepreneur, one of the most critical skills you can learn is how to manage your team effectively. Your team is the backbone of your business, and they are the ones who will help you bring your vision to life. But managing a team can be challenging, especially when dealing with creative individuals who have their unique ways of working. In this chapter, we will discuss some tips and tricks for managing your team effectively.

Communication is key

The most critical aspect of managing a team is communication. You need to communicate your vision, goals, and expectations clearly to your team. This will ensure that everyone is on the same page and working towards a common goal. Encourage your team members to communicate with each other as well, as this will help build a sense of teamwork and collaboration.

Set clear goals and expectations

As an entrepreneur, you need to set clear goals and expectations for your team. This will help them understand what they need to achieve and how they need to do it. Be specific about deadlines, deliverables, and milestones. This will help your team members stay focused and motivated.

Encourage creativity

Creative entrepreneurship is all about innovation and creativity. Encourage your team members to think outside the box and come up with new ideas and solutions. This will help your business stay ahead of the competition and keep things fresh and exciting for your customers.

Provide feedback

Feedback is essential for growth and improvement. Provide your team members with regular feedback on their performance. This will help them understand what they are doing well and where they need to improve. Be constructive in your feedback, and always provide suggestions for improvement.

Celebrate successes

Finally, celebrate your team's successes. Recognise their hard work and accomplishments, and show them that you appreciate their efforts. This will help build morale and motivate your team to continue working hard.

Managing a team takes practice and patience, but by following these tips, you can create a productive and successful team that will help you achieve your business goals. Remember, your team is your most valuable asset, so invest in them, and they will help you build a thriving business.

MARKETING YOUR BUSINESS

Creating a Marketing Strategy

MARKETING is an essential component of any business. Without it, your business will struggle to reach its target audience and generate sales. That's why it's crucial to develop a marketing strategy that aligns with your business goals and objectives.

A marketing strategy is a comprehensive plan that outlines how you will promote your products or services to your target audience. It includes everything from identifying your target market and understanding their needs to selecting the right channels to reach them and measuring the success of your marketing efforts.

Here are the essential steps to creating a marketing strategy:

1. **Define your target audience:** Identify the people who are most likely to purchase your products or services. Consider factors such as age, gender, location, income level, and interests.

2. **Understand their needs:** Once you've identified your target audience,

conduct research to understand their pain points and what motivates them to make a purchase.

3. **Develop a unique value proposition:** Your unique value proposition is what sets you apart from your competitors. It's a statement that communicates the unique benefits of your products or services to your target audience.

4. **Set your marketing goals:** Your marketing goals should align with your business objectives. For example, if your goal is to increase sales, your marketing goal may be to generate more leads.

5. **Select your marketing channels:** There are various marketing channels you can use to reach your target audience, such as social media, email marketing, search engine optimisation (SEO), and paid advertising. Select the channels that are most likely to resonate with your target audience.

6. **Develop a content plan:** Your content plan should include the types of content you will create, the topics you will cover, and the frequency of your content. Ensure that your content is valuable and relevant to your target audience.

7. **Measure your success:** Track and measure the success of your marketing efforts. Use data to refine and improve your marketing strategy over time.

In conclusion, creating a marketing strategy is critical to the success of your business. By understanding your target audience, developing a unique value proposition, setting your marketing goals, selecting your marketing channels, developing a content plan, and measuring your success, you can create a marketing strategy that drives business growth and success.

Identifying Your Target Market

ONE of the most important aspects of running a successful business is identifying your target market. Without a clear understanding of who your ideal customer is, it can be difficult to create a product or service that resonates with them. As a creative entrepreneur, you have the added challenge of appealing to a niche audience, making it even more important to identify and understand your target market.

First, consider the demographics of your ideal customer. What age range, gender, income level, and education level are they likely to have? Are they located in a specific geographic region? Understanding these basic demographics can help you tailor your marketing efforts and product offerings to better appeal to your target market.

Next, consider the psychographics of your ideal customer. What are their interests, values, and beliefs? What motivates them to make a purchase? Understanding these factors can help you create a product or service that speaks to their needs and desires.

It's also important to consider your competition when identifying your target market. Who are they targeting and how can you differentiate your product or service to appeal to a different segment of the market? Additionally, consider the size of your potential market and whether it's large enough to support your business.

Once you've identified your target market, it's important to continually evaluate and refine your understanding. As your business grows and evolves, your target market may change as well. Keep an eye on trends and shifts in your industry and adjust your marketing and product offerings accordingly.

In summary, identifying your target market is essential to the success of any business, particularly in the realm of creative entrepreneurship. By understanding the demographics and Psychographics of your ideal customer, as well as your competition and potential market size, you can create a product or service that speaks directly to the needs and desires of your target market. Continually evaluating and refining your understanding of your target market can help ensure long-term success for your business.

Building Your Brand

AS a creative entrepreneur, building your brand is crucial to the success of your business. Your brand is what sets you apart from your competitors and helps you to connect with your target audience. It's more than just a logo or a name – it's the essence of your business and what it stands for.

The first step in building your brand is to define what you want to be known for. This means identifying your unique selling proposition (USP) and understanding your target audience. Your USP is what makes your business different from others in your industry. It could be your product, your customer service, or your values and beliefs. Once you have identified your USP, you can start to develop your brand around it.

Your brand should be consistent across all your marketing materials, from your website to your social media profiles. This includes your logo, colour scheme, and tone of voice. Consistency helps to reinforce your brand and build trust with your audience.

Another important aspect of building your brand is to create a strong visual identity. This includes your logo, business cards, and any other visual materials that represent your business. Your visual identity should be memorable and reflect your brand's personality.

In addition to your visual identity, you should also focus on your brand's messaging. This includes your tag line, mission statement, and any other messaging that communicates your brand's values and beliefs. Your messaging should be consistent with your visual identity and USP.

Finally, building your brand requires ongoing effort and investment. You should regularly review your brand strategy and make adjustments as needed. This could include updating your visual identity or refining your messaging. It's also important to invest in marketing and advertising to raise awareness of your brand and attract new customers.

In conclusion, building your brand is an essential component of creative entrepreneurship. It requires a clear understanding of your USP and target audience, consistency in your visual identity and messaging, and ongoing effort and investment. By focusing on these key elements, you can create a strong brand that sets you apart from your competitors and resonates with your audience.

MANAGING YOUR FINANCES

Financial Management Basics

AS an entrepreneur, it is important to understand the basics of financial management. Managing your finances well can make or break your business, and can determine whether your creative ideas become successful ventures. Here are some fundamentals to keep in mind:

Understand your finances

The first step to effective financial management is to understand your finances. This means tracking your income and expenses, understanding your profit margins, and keeping an eye on your cash flow. It is important to have a clear understanding of your financial situation so that you can make informed decisions about your business.

Create a budget

Creating a budget is an essential part of financial management. A budget helps you to plan your expenses and make sure that you have enough money to cover your costs. It also helps you to set financial goals and track your progress towards achieving them.

Monitor your cash flow

Cash flow is the lifeblood of any business. It is important to monitor your cash flow regularly to ensure that you have enough money to cover your expenses. This means tracking your accounts receivable and accounts payable, and making sure that you are collecting payments on time.

Manage your debt

Debt can be a useful tool for growing your business, but it can also be a burden if not managed properly. It is important to have a clear understanding of your debt obligations and to make sure that you are making payments on time. You should also avoid taking on more debt than you can handle.

Invest wisely

Investing in your business can help to fuel growth and increase profitability. However, it is important to invest wisely and to avoid taking on too much risk. You should also make sure that you have a clear understanding of the potential return on investment before making any financial decisions.

In conclusion, financial management is an essential part of running a successful business. By understanding your finances, creating a budget, monitoring your cash flow, managing your debt, and investing wisely, you can ensure that your creative ideas become successful ventures.

Budgeting and Forecasting

BUDGETING and forecasting are essential components of creative entrepreneurship. As an entrepreneur, you need to plan and strategise for your business's future by creating an accurate budget and forecast. This chapter will provide you with an in-depth understanding of budgeting and forecasting and how to implement these practices to achieve business success.

Budgeting is the process of creating a financial plan for your business. It involves estimating your income, expenses, and profits for a specific period, usually a year. Budgeting helps you to identify your business's financial needs and allocate resources effectively. It also enables you to set financial goals and measure your progress against them.

To create a budget, you need to have a clear understanding of your business's financial history and current performance. You should also consider your business's goals and objectives, market trends, and economic factors that could affect your business's financial performance.

Forecasting, on the other hand, is the process of predicting your business's future financial performance. It involves analysing past performance data, market trends, and economic factors to predict your business's revenue, expenses, and profits for a specific period, usually a year or more.

Forecasting helps you to identify potential financial opportunities and risks, enabling you to make informed business decisions. It also helps you to plan for future expenses and investments, ensuring that you have enough resources to achieve your business goals.

To create an accurate forecast, you need to have a clear understanding of your business's financial history, market trends, and economic factors that could affect your business's financial performance. You should also consider your business's goals and objectives and plan for future expenses and investments.

In conclusion, budgeting and forecasting are critical practices for creative entrepreneurship. By creating an accurate budget and forecast, you can plan and strategise for your business's future, identify financial opportunities and risks, and make informed business decisions. As an entrepreneur, you should prioritise budgeting and forecasting to achieve business success.

Managing Cash Flow

AS a creative entrepreneur, managing cash flow is vital to the success of your business. Cash flow is the movement of money in and out of your business, and it is essential to keep it balanced and steady. In this subchapter, we will discuss the importance of managing cash flow and provide you with tips on how to maintain a healthy financial status.

Why is Managing Cash Flow Important?

Cash flow management is crucial because it affects the overall financial health of your business. Poor cash flow management can lead to insolvency, which is one of the primary reasons why businesses fail. For creative entrepreneurs, this is especially relevant because many businesses are funded by personal savings or loans, making cash flow management even more critical.

Tips for Managing Cash Flow

Create a Budget

Creating a budget is the first step in managing your cash flow. A budget helps you plan and keep track of your expenses and revenue, allowing you to identify cash flow problems in advance. It's essential to stick to your budget and adjust it as necessary.

Monitor Your Cash Flow Regularly

Monitoring your cash flow on a regular basis helps you identify potential issues early. It enables you to make informed decisions about your business and helps you plan for the future. Make sure to track your expenses and revenue, and keep an eye on your accounts receivable and payable.

Manage Your Accounts Receivable

Managing your accounts receivable is critical to maintaining a healthy cash flow. Ensure that you invoice your clients promptly and follow up on any overdue payments. You may also want to consider offering incentives for early payments or charging interest on late payments.

Control Your Expenses

Controlling your expenses is essential to maintaining a positive cash flow. Keep an eye on your expenses and look for ways to reduce them where possible. You may want to consider negotiating better rates with your suppliers or cutting back on non-essential expenses.

Conclusion

Managing cash flow is vital for the success of your creative entrepreneurship venture. By creating a budget, monitoring your cash flow, managing your accounts receivable, and controlling your expenses, you can maintain a healthy financial status and grow your business. Remember to stay on top of your finances and make informed decisions to ensure the longevity of your business.

SCALING YOUR BUSINESS

Knowing When to Scale

AS a creative entrepreneur, one of the most important things you need to know is when to scale your business. Scaling means taking your business to the next level, expanding your operations, and increasing your revenue.

Scaling is not an easy process, and it requires a lot of effort, time, and resources. However, if done correctly, it can lead to significant growth and success for your business.

So, how do you know when to scale your business? Here are some signs that indicate it may be time to take the leap:

Demand for your product or service is increasing

If you are seeing a steady increase in demand for your product or service, it may be a sign that it's time to scale. This means that there is a market for your business, and you have the potential to grow your customer base and revenue.

Your business is profitable

If your business is profitable and generating a steady stream of income, it may be time to consider scaling. This means that you have the financial resources to invest in the growth of your business.

You have a solid team in place

Scaling your business requires a strong team to support it. If you have a solid team in place that can handle the increased workload, it may be a sign that it's time to scale.

You have a clear vision for the future

Scaling your business requires a clear vision for the future. If you have a plan in place for how you want to grow your business and what you want to achieve, it may be time to take the next step.

You are ready to take on new challenges

Scaling your business is not easy, and it requires a willingness to take on new challenges. If you are ready to step out of your comfort zone and tackle new obstacles, it may be a sign that it's time to scale.

In conclusion, scaling your business is an important decision that requires careful consideration and planning. However, if you are seeing signs that indicate it may be time to take the next step, it's worth exploring the possibilities of growth and success that come with scaling.

Growing Your Business Strategically

AS a creative entrepreneur, you may have started your business with a vision and a passion for your craft. However, as your business grows, it's important to have a strategic plan in place to sustain and expand your success.

One of the first steps in growing your business strategically is to assess your current situation. Take a look at your finances, your customer base, and your competition. Identify any gaps or areas of improvement that need to be addressed in order to reach your goals.

Next, develop a clear and measurable plan for growth. This may involve expanding your product or service offerings, increasing your marketing efforts, or improving your operational efficiency. Whatever your plan entails, make sure it aligns with your overall vision and values as a business.

In order to execute your plan effectively, it's important to prioritise and focus on the most critical areas of your business. This may mean delegating tasks to employees or outsourcing certain functions to experts in the field. By focusing on your strengths and delegating tasks that are not your forte, you can optimise your time and resources for maximum impact.

Another key element of strategic growth is building strong partnerships and collaborations. Look for opportunities to partner with other businesses or optimise that share your values and can help you reach new audiences or expand your reach. This can also include collaborating with influencers or thought leaders in your industry to increase your visibility and credibility.

Finally, be prepared to adapt and pivot as needed. The business landscape is constantly evolving, and it's important to be flexible and responsive to changes in the market or shifts in consumer preferences. By staying nimble and open to new opportunities, you can position your business for long-term success.

In summary, growing your business strategically involves assessing your current situation, developing a clear plan for growth, prioritising your resources, building strong partnerships, and being adaptable to change. By taking a holistic and intentional approach to growth, you can sustain and expand your success as a creative entrepreneur.

Managing the Challenges of Growth

AS a creative entrepreneur, your ultimate goal is to grow your business. However, with growth comes a new set of challenges that can be difficult to navigate. Here are some tips for managing the challenges of growth:

Stay focused on your core values and mission

As your business grows, it can be tempting to chase after new opportunities that may not align with your core values and mission. However, it's important to stay focused on what's important to you and your business. Remember why you started your business in the first place and make sure that all new opportunities align with your mission.

Hire the right people

As your business grows, you'll need to hire more employees to help you manage the workload. It's important to hire people who share your vision and are a good fit for your company culture. Take the time to find the right people, and invest in their training and development.

Be flexible

As your business grows, you'll encounter new challenges and opportunities that you may not have anticipated. It's important to be flexible and willing to adapt to new situations. Be open to new ideas and be willing to pivot your business strategy if necessary.

Manage cash flow

As your business grows, your expenses will increase, and you'll need to manage your cash flow carefully. Make sure you have a solid financial management plan in place, and monitor your cash flow regularly. Consider working with a financial advisor to help you manage your finances.

Stay connected to your customers

As your business grows, it can be easy to lose touch with your customers. Make sure you stay connected to your customers by seeking their feedback and engaging with them on social media. This will help you stay in tune with their needs and preferences, and enable you to continue to deliver products and services that meet their needs.

Managing the challenges of growth can be difficult, but with the right mindset and strategies, you can successfully navigate these challenges and build a thriving business. Remember to stay focused on your core values, hire the right people, be flexible, manage cash flow, and stay connected to your customers.

THE ALCHEMY OF BUSINESS

The Exciting Journey

BEING an entrepreneur can be exhilarating, yet it comes with its own set of challenges and risks.

According to the latest data, up to 90% of startups fail. Across almost all industries, the average failure rate for year one is 10%. However, in years two through five, a staggering 70% of new businesses will fail. Let's understand: Approximately 30% of new small businesses fail by the end of year two, while half will fail before year five. That means roughly 70% of startups fail within their first five years of operations. Speaking globally, on average, 63% of tech startups don't make it, 25% close down during the first year, and only 10% survive in the long run. Venture-backed fintech startups fail in 75% of cases. A recap in terms of conservative estimates: 30% of startups fail within three years, 50% don't make it past five years, and 70% close down in 10 years. Only 40% manage to turn a profit.

It is clear that the entrepreneurial journey is no bed of roses. The time spent is significant in an individual's professional life. This period is not only crucial but also precious from an individual's perspective. If you accept the situation positively, then the time spent is an experiment, worthwhile, and a lesson well learned. Should a business fail before it really takes off, it takes a lot of courage to get things back on track. However, those who overcome these challenges have created a lasting impact and made money while making a difference. Let's discuss what it takes to be a Creative Entrepreneur.

In the realm of commerce, where strategy meets opportunity and innovation blends with perseverance, lies a transformative force known as "The Alchemy of Business." Much like the ancient pursuit of turning base metals into gold, mastering the dynamics of business requires a blend of artistry, precision, and vision. It is a symphony where ideas harmonise with execution, where challenges are catalysts for growth, and where resilience is the philosopher's stone that turns setbacks into successes.

At its core, the alchemy of business is about more than mere profitability; it is the art of turning dreams into realities, of navigating uncertainty with unwavering determination, and of creating value that transcends mere monetary gain. It is a journey that demands not just knowledge but wisdom, not just ambition but integrity. Every entrepreneur, every visionary who has dared to challenge the status quo and build something extraordinary has engaged in this alchemy, forging their own path through the crucible of enterprise.

Read on as we delve into the secrets of "The Alchemy of Business," exploring how inspiration transforms into innovation, how leadership refines the raw materials of potential, and how each decision, each action, contributes to the grand experiment of building something enduring and impactful. Together, let's uncover the principles that turn ideas into empires and aspirations into achievements.

Traits of Creative Entrepreneurs

- **Visionary Thinking**: Ability to see possibilities beyond the current state.
- **Risk-taking**: Willingness to take calculated risks to innovate.
- **Adaptability**: Flexibility to pivot and adjust strategies as needed.
- **Passion**: Deep enthusiasm and dedication to their ideas and goals.
- **Problem-solving**: Capacity to identify problems and devise innovative solutions.
- **Resourcefulness**: Ability to make the most of limited resources.
- **Resilience**: Persistence and ability to bounce back from setbacks.
- **Networking**: Skill in building and leveraging relationships.
- **Open-mindedness**: Willingness to consider unconventional ideas.
- **Curiosity**: Constantly seeking new knowledge and insights.
- **Creativity**: Capacity to think outside the box and generate novel ideas.
- **Self-confidence**: Belief in one's abilities and ideas.
- **Customer-focused**: Prioritising understanding and meeting customer needs.
- **Leadership**: Inspiring and guiding others towards shared goals.
- **Continuous Learning**: Commitment to personal and professional growth.
- **Adaptive Communication**: Ability to convey ideas effectively to different audiences.
- **Financial Literacy**: Understanding of financial management and budgeting.
- **Ethical Awareness**: Consideration of ethical implications in business decisions.
- **Global Perspective**: Awareness of international markets and trends.

- **Team Building**: Capacity to attract and motivate talented individuals.

These traits collectively define the mindset and capabilities of a creative entrepreneur, enabling them to navigate challenges and capitalise on opportunities in dynamic business environments. A good entrepreneur has leadership, creativity, ability to network, risk-taking, determination, adaptability, optimism, vision, empathy, flexibility, perseverance, a strong work ethic, effective communication, resilience, time management, willingness to accept failure, and above all, tenacity. These qualities contribute to their ability to innovate, overcome obstacles, and lead successful ventures. Successful entrepreneurs are disciplined, self-motivating, adaptable, determined, organised, patient, have a sound knowledge of their product or service and that of their industry domain.

Tactics to Develop Creative Entrepreneurship in Today's Entrepreneurs

DEVELOPING creative entrepreneurship in today's entrepreneurs involves fostering a mindset that encourages innovation, risk-taking, and strategic thinking. Here are several methods to achieve this:

1. **Encourage Experimentation and Risk-Taking:**
   - Create an environment where entrepreneurs feel safe to experiment with new ideas and take calculated risks.
   - Emphasise that failures are learning opportunities rather than setbacks.

2. **Promote Cross-Disciplinary Thinking:**
   - Encourage entrepreneurs to draw inspiration from diverse fields

and industries.

- Foster collaboration between individuals with different backgrounds and expertise to generate novel ideas.

3. **Provide Access to Resources and Support:**
   - Offer access to mentors, networks, and resources such as funding, incubators, and accelerators.
   - Provide workshops and training sessions on creative problem-solving, design thinking, and innovation frameworks.

4. **Cultivate a Culture of Innovation:**
   - Foster a culture that values and rewards creativity and innovation.
   - Recognise and celebrate entrepreneurial successes and breakthroughs.

5. **Emphasise Customer-Centric Innovation:**
   - Encourage entrepreneurs to deeply understand customer needs and pain points.
   - Prioritise developing solutions that address these needs in unique and effective ways.

6. **Support Continuous Learning:**
   - Promote ongoing education and skill development in areas such as technology, marketing, and business management.
   - Encourage entrepreneurs to stay updated on industry trends and emerging technologies.

7. **Stimulate Curiosity and Vision:**
   - Inspire entrepreneurs to think beyond current trends and envision future possibilities.
   - Encourage them to question assumptions and explore unconven-

tional ideas.

8. **Facilitate Networking and Collaboration:**
- Provide opportunities for entrepreneurs to connect with peers, industry leaders, investors, and potential collaborators.
- Foster a community where knowledge sharing and collaboration are encouraged.

9. **Encourage Ethical and Sustainable Practices:**
- Promote entrepreneurship that considers ethical implications and contributes positively to society.
- Support initiatives that prioritise sustainability and social responsibility.

10. **Measure and Adapt:**
- Establish metrics to assess the effectiveness of initiatives aimed at fostering creative entrepreneurship.
- Continuously gather feedback and adjust strategies based on results and evolving needs.

By implementing these methods, organisations and communities can effectively nurture creative entrepreneurship among today's entrepreneurs, fostering innovation and driving economic and societal growth.

Entrepreneurship Vision in Today's Entrepreneurs

CREATING an entrepreneurship vision in today's entrepreneurs involves inspiring and guiding them towards a clear purpose and long-term goals. Here are some effective methods to foster and develop an entrepreneurship vision:

1. **Purpose and Passion Alignment:** Help entrepreneurs connect their personal values and passions with their business idea. Encourage them to think deeply about why they want to start a business and how it aligns with their values.

2. **Visualising Success:** Guide entrepreneurs to visualise what success looks like for them and their business. This could include imagining their business in 5 or 10 years, the impact they want to create, and the legacy they want to leave behind.

3. **Setting Clear Goals:** Assist entrepreneurs in setting specific, measurable, achievable, relevant, and time-bound (SMART) goals. These goals should reflect their long-term vision and provide a road map for their entrepreneurial journey.

4. **Identifying Challenges and Opportunities:** Help entrepreneurs analyse market trends, identify potential challenges, and recognise opportunities within their industry. This helps them develop a strategic vision that anticipates future developments.

5. **Creating a Mission Statement:** Guide entrepreneurs in crafting a mission statement that encapsulates their vision and values. A strong mission statement can serve as a guiding light during difficult times and inspire stakeholders.

6. **Mentorship and Role Models:** Connect entrepreneurs with mentors who have successfully realised their own visions. Learning from others' experiences and successes can provide valuable insights and inspiration.

7. **Encouraging Innovation and Creativity:** Foster an environment that encourages experimentation, innovation, and creative problem-solving. Entrepreneurs should feel empowered to think outside the box and explore new ideas that align with their vision.

8. **Building a Support Network:** Help entrepreneurs build a network of supporters, advisors, and collaborators who can provide guidance, feedback, and encouragement along their entrepreneurial journey.

9. **Continuous Learning and Adaptation:** Emphasise the importance of continuous learning and adaptation. The entrepreneurial landscape is constantly evolving, and successful entrepreneurs are those who can pivot when necessary while staying true to their long-term vision.

10. **Celebrating Milestones:** Celebrate achievements and milestones along the way. Recognising progress can reinforce commitment to the vision and inspire continued effort.

By employing these methods, aspiring entrepreneurs can develop a clear and compelling entrepreneurship vision that guides their decisions, motivates their team, and attracts stakeholders who share their passion and purpose.

How Can Creative Entrepreneurs Build a Vision of their Brand

BUILDING a brand takes time like Rome was not built in a day. Absolutely right! Building a brand requires patience, persistence, and consistent effort over time. Just like Rome, which took centuries to become the iconic city it is today, establishing a brand that stands out and resonates with people takes time and dedication. Each step you take in building your brand contributes to its strength and recognition, much like each stone laid in the foundation of Rome contributed to its grandeur.

Building a vision for a brand is crucial for creative entrepreneurs. Here are some steps they can take to develop a strong vision:

1. **Define Your Purpose:** Understand why your brand exists beyond making money. What problem does it solve? What values does it embody?

2. **Identify Your Target Audience:** Who are your ideal customers? What are their needs, desires, and pain points? Tailor your vision to resonate with them.

3. **Craft Your Unique Selling Proposition (USP):** What sets your brand apart from competitors? Define what makes your offering unique and valuable.

4. **Create a Brand Story:** Develop a narrative that communicates your brand's history, mission, and values. Make it compelling and authentic.

5. **Visualise Your Brand Identity:** Design a visual representation of your

brand through logos, colours, typography, and imagery that aligns with your vision.

6. **Set Long-Term Goals:** Define where you want your brand to be in the future. Establish measurable objectives that guide your growth and development.

7. **Consistency Across Platforms:** Ensure that your brand's vision is consistent across all touch points — website, social media, products, customer service, etc.

8. **Seek Feedback and Iterate:** Gather input from customers, peers, and mentors to refine your brand vision. Continuously adapt and improve based on insights.

9. **Stay True to Your Values:** Uphold the core values and principles that define your brand, even as you adapt to changes in the market.

10. **Inspire and Lead:** As the entrepreneur, embody your brand's vision in your actions and decisions. Inspire others — employees, customers, and partners — to align with your brand's purpose and mission.

By following these steps, creative entrepreneurs can build a clear and compelling vision for their brand, setting a solid foundation for growth and success.

Creative Entrepreneurship of Azim Premji

Azim Premji, the Indian business tycoon and philanthropist, is known for his transformative impact on the IT industry and his approach to creative entrepreneurship. Here are some key aspects of his journey:

Early Years and Entrepreneurial Spirit: Azim Premji took over his family's vegetable oil business, Western India Vegetable Products, in 1966 at the age of 21, after the sudden death of his father. This marked the beginning of his entrepreneurial journey.

Transformation of Wipro: Under Azim Premji's leadership, Western India Vegetable Products (Wipro) diversified from edible oils into IT services. He foresaw the potential of the burgeoning computer industry in the 1970s and shifted Wipro's focus towards software development and IT services.

Strategic Vision: Premji's strategic vision was pivotal in positioning Wipro as a global IT services company. He emphasised quality, customer-centricity, and innovation, which are essential aspects of creative entrepreneurship.

Adaptability and Innovation: Creative entrepreneurship often involves adapting to changing market dynamics and innovating to stay ahead. Premji navigated Wipro through various economic and technological shifts, continuously innovating in service offerings and business models.

Philanthropy and Social Impact: In 2001, Azim Premji founded the Azim Premji Foundation, focused on improving education in India. This reflects his belief in using wealth for social good, a characteristic often seen in creative entrepreneurs who aim to make a positive impact beyond profits.

Legacy: Azim Premji's legacy extends beyond business success; it encompasses his contributions to education, social development, and ethical business practices. His approach to entrepreneurship emphasises long-term sustainability, ethical governance, and social responsibility.

In summary, Azim Premji exemplifies creative entrepreneurship through his strategic foresight, innovation, adaptability, and commitment to social impact. His journey with Wipro and the Azim Premji Foundation serves as a testament to the power of entrepreneurship not just for profit, but for driving positive change in society.

> *Excellence is a great starting point for any new organisation but also an unending journey. The three ordinary things that we often don't pay enough attention to, but which I believe are the drivers of all success, are hard work, perseverance, and basic honesty.*
> *— Azim Premji*

If there's ONLY one lesson you can learn from Azim Premji, it is: "perseverance in pursuing growth and innovation."

Creative Entrepreneurship of Ratan Tata

Ratan Tata is known not only for his business acumen but also for his innovative approach to entrepreneurship. Here are some aspects that showcase his creative entrepreneurship:

Visionary Leadership: Ratan Tata was known for his long-term vision and strategic foresight. Under his leadership, Tata Group expanded globally, acquiring iconic brands like Jaguar Land Rover, Tetley, and Corus Steel, which diversified and strengthened the group's portfolio.

Social Responsibility: Tata infused a strong sense of social responsibility into the business ethos of Tata Group. Initiatives like Tata Nano, the world's cheapest car aimed at providing affordable transportation to millions in India, and the Tata Swach, a low-cost water purifier, demonstrated his commitment to addressing social issues through innovative products.

Support for Innovation: Ratan Tata encouraged innovation within the Tata Group by fostering an entrepreneurial spirit among employees. He supported initiatives like the Tata Innovation Fellowship and the Tata Nano Excellence Center to nurture innovation and R&D capabilities within the organisation.

Investment in Startups: After retiring as Chairman of Tata Sons, Ratan Tata became actively involved in the startup ecosystem in India. He set up Tata Opportunities Fund to invest in promising startups across various sectors, thereby supporting and promoting entrepreneurship in the country.

Adaptability and Resilience: During his tenure, Ratan Tata navigated through various challenges including economic downturns and global competition. His ability to adapt to changing business landscapes while staying true to the core values of Tata Group underscores his resilience as a leader.

Global Expansion: Under Ratan Tata's leadership, Tata Group significantly expanded its global footprint. Acquiring well-established international brands not only diversified the group's revenue streams but also positioned Tata as a global player in industries ranging from steel and automotive to beverages and IT services.

Philanthropy and Corporate Governance: Ratan Tata emphasised the importance of ethical practices and corporate governance within Tata Group. His commitment to philanthropy led to the establishment of Tata

Trusts, which focus on various social development initiatives including healthcare, education, and rural livelihoods.

Ratan Tata's legacy as a creative entrepreneur is marked by his ability to blend business success with social impact, foster innovation, and navigate challenges with resilience and foresight. His approach continues to inspire aspiring entrepreneurs and business leaders globally.

> *If you want to walk fast, walk alone. But if you want to walk far, walk together.*
> — *Ratan Tata*

If there's ONLY one lesson you can learn from Ratan Tata, it is: "Build a Brand That's Trustworthy."

Creative Entrepreneurship of Elon Musk

Elon Musk is a fascinating example of creative entrepreneurship, known for his ambitious ventures that span multiple industries. Here's a breakdown of his approach and some key ventures:

Vision and Approach

1. Ambitious Goals: Musk is driven by audacious goals aimed at solving some of humanity's biggest challenges, such as climate change and space exploration.

2. Technological Innovation: He leverages cutting-edge technology to disrupt traditional industries and push boundaries.

3. Risk-taking: Musk is known for taking significant risks, both financially and technologically, to achieve his visions.

Key Ventures

1. Tesla, Inc.: Revolutionising the automotive industry with electric vehicles (EVs) that are both sustainable and high-performance.

2. SpaceX: Redefining space travel with reusable rockets, aiming to make space exploration more affordable and accessible.

3. SolarCity (now Tesla Energy): Promoting sustainable energy solutions through solar power and energy storage systems.

4. Neuralink: Advancing brain-computer interface technology to potentially enhance human cognition and address neurological diseases.

5. The Boring Company: Innovating tunnel construction technology to alleviate urban congestion and transform transportation.

Entrepreneurial Strategies

1. Vertical Integration: Musk often integrates multiple stages of production and distribution within a single company (e.g., Tesla manufacturing its own batteries).

2. Iterative Development: Companies like SpaceX emphasise rapid prototyping and iterative design to accelerate innovation cycles.

3. Public Engagement: Musk engages with the public and potential customers via social media, generating excitement and feedback.

Challenges and Criticisms

1. Financial Strain: Some ventures, like SpaceX in its early years, faced financial difficulties before achieving profitability.

2. Work-Life Balance: Musk's intense work ethic and demanding schedules have sparked concerns about burnout.

Impact and Legacy

1. Industry Disruption: Musk's ventures have disrupted established industries and forced competitors to innovate.

2. Inspiration: He serves as an inspiration for entrepreneurs globally, encouraging bold thinking and ambitious goals.

Elon Musk's creative entrepreneurship is characterised by his bold vision, technological prowess, and a relentless pursuit of innovation. His ventures continue to shape the future of transportation, energy, and space exploration, leaving a profound impact on industries and inspiring the next generation of entrepreneurs.

Creative Entrepreneurship of Jeff Bezos

Jeff Bezos is often cited as a quintessential example of creative entrepreneurship, primarily due to his founding and leadership of Amazon.com. Here are some key aspects of Jeff Bezos's approach to creative entrepreneurship:

1. **Visionary Leadership:** Bezos started Amazon in 1994 with the

vision of creating an online marketplace that could sell everything. His foresight into the potential of e-commerce revolutionised retail and set the stage for Amazon to become a global powerhouse.

2. **Customer-Centric Innovation:** Bezos famously prioritised long-term customer satisfaction over short-term profits. This philosophy drove Amazon's relentless focus on improving customer experience through innovations like one-click ordering, personalised recommendations, and Prime membership benefits.

3. **Risk-Taking and Innovation:** Bezos has been known for his willingness to take risks and embrace innovation. Amazon diversified beyond books early on, expanding into areas such as electronics, cloud computing (Amazon Web Services), and even space exploration (Blue Origin).

4. **Disruptive Business Models:** Amazon disrupted traditional retail models by leveraging technology to streamline operations and reduce costs, which allowed the company to offer competitive pricing and fast shipping options.

5. **Long-Term Thinking:** Bezos is a proponent of thinking long-term and investing heavily in future growth opportunities. This is evident in Amazon's strategy of reinvesting profits into expanding its infrastructure, developing new technologies, and entering new markets.

6. **Culture of Innovation:** Under Bezos's leadership, Amazon fostered a culture that encourages experimentation and embraces failure as a necessary part of innovation. This has led to the creation of new products and services such as the Kindle e-reader and Alexa-powered devices.

7. **Adaptability and Flexibility:** Bezos has demonstrated the ability to adapt and evolve Amazon's business model in response to changing market dynamics and consumer behaviour. This flexibility has been key to Amazon's sustained growth and dominance in multiple industries.

8. **Global Impact:** Amazon's global reach and influence have reshaped not just retail but also logistics, cloud computing, and digital entertainment. Bezos's entrepreneurial journey with Amazon has inspired countless startups and entrepreneurs worldwide.

Jeff Bezos exemplifies creative entrepreneurship through his visionary leadership, customer-centric approach, risk-taking mentality, and relentless pursuit of innovation. His legacy with Amazon continues to shape the landscape of business and technology, making him a compelling case study in entrepreneurial success.

Creative Entrepreneurship of Larry Ellison

Larry Ellison, the co-founder of Oracle Corporation, is a notable figure in the realm of creative entrepreneurship. His journey is characterised by several key elements that define his approach to business and innovation:

Visionary Leadership

Ellison demonstrated visionary leadership by recognising early on the potential of relational databases and the significance of data management in the emerging field of computer technology. His vision laid the foundation for Oracle's growth and dominance in the database software industry.

Innovation and Technological Prowess

Ellison's entrepreneurship is deeply rooted in innovation. Under his guidance, Oracle pioneered many technological advancements in database systems, such as the development of the first commercially available SQL-based relational database management system. This commitment to technological innovation positioned Oracle as a leader in enterprise software solutions.

Strategic Acquisitions and Expansion

Ellison employed a strategy of strategic acquisitions to expand Oracle's capabilities and market reach. Notable acquisitions include Sun Microsystems, which bolstered Oracle's position in hardware and software integration, and PeopleSoft, which strengthened Oracle's enterprise applications portfolio.

Competitive Spirit and Risk-Taking

Ellison is known for his competitive spirit and willingness to take risks. He famously challenged industry giants like IBM and Microsoft, often leading Oracle into direct competition with these established players. His boldness and confidence in Oracle's technology and team have been crucial to the company's growth and resilience in the competitive tech landscape.

Philanthropy and Social Impact

Beyond business, Ellison has also engaged in philanthropic efforts, focusing on education, healthcare, and wildlife conservation through the Ellison Medical Foundation and the Lawrence Ellison Foundation.

His philanthropy reflects a commitment to making a positive impact beyond the realm of technology.

Personal Style and Influence

Ellison's personal style is characterised by a charismatic and sometimes controversial demeanour. His leadership has been instrumental in shaping Oracle's corporate culture and business strategy, emphasising agility, innovation, and customer-centricity.

Larry Ellison's creative entrepreneurship is marked by visionary leadership, technological innovation, strategic acquisitions, competitive spirit, philanthropy, and a distinctive personal influence. These elements have not only shaped Oracle Corporation but also left a lasting impact on the technology industry as a whole.

Creative Entrepreneurship of Larry Page And Sergey Brin

Larry Page and Sergey Brin, the co-founders of Google, exemplify creative entrepreneurship through their innovative approach to solving problems and their ambitious vision for the future of technology. Here are some key aspects of their journey:

1. **Innovative Search Technology:** Page and Brin developed Google's core technology while they were still students at Stanford University. Their PageRank algorithm revolutionised web search by ranking search results based on relevance, rather than just keyword matching.

2. **Ambitious Vision:** From the beginning, Page and Brin envisioned

Google not just as a search engine, but as a company that could organise the world's information and make it universally accessible and useful. This vision has guided Google's expansion into various products and services beyond search.

3. **Entrepreneurial Spirit:** They demonstrated a strong entrepreneurial spirit by founding Google in a garage in 1998, and later successfully scaling it into one of the most influential technology companies in the world. Their ability to attract top talent and manage rapid growth was crucial to Google's success.

4. **Innovation in Advertising:** Google's AdWords platform, developed by Page and Brin, revolutionised online advertising by allowing businesses to target ads based on user searches. This innovation not only fuelled Google's revenue growth but also changed the digital advertising landscape.

5. **Commitment to Innovation:** Even after Google became a household name, Page and Brin continued to foster a culture of innovation within the company. They encouraged moonshot projects through Google X (now X), which aimed to tackle major global issues through technology.

6. **Alphabet Inc.:** In 2015, Page and Brin restructured Google into Alphabet Inc., a conglomerate overseeing various businesses including Google, Waymo (self-driving cars), Verily (life sciences), and others. This move allowed them to focus on long-term innovation while maintaining Google's dominance in search and advertising.

7. **Philanthropy and Impact:** Through their personal philanthropic efforts and initiatives like Google.org, Page and Brin have aimed to use technology to address global challenges, such as climate change and

healthcare.

Larry Page and Sergey Brin's journey as entrepreneurs is marked by their relentless pursuit of innovation, their transformative impact on the internet and technology sectors, and their commitment to using their success to make a positive difference in the world. Their story continues to inspire entrepreneurs and innovators globally to think big and strive for meaningful impact through creativity and entrepreneurship.

Creative Entrepreneurship of Michael Dell

Michael Dell is a prominent figure in the realm of creative entrepreneurship, having founded Dell Technologies in 1984 at the age of 19. His entrepreneurial journey is marked by several key creative and strategic decisions:

1. **Direct Sales Model:** One of Dell's most innovative contributions was the direct sales model. By selling directly to customers and customising orders, Dell bypassed the traditional distribution channels, reducing costs and allowing for more personalised products.

2. **Build-to-Order Approach:** Dell pioneered the build-to-order approach in the computer industry. Instead of producing computers and storing them in inventory, Dell started manufacturing only after receiving orders. This not only minimised inventory costs but also ensured that customers received the latest technology.

3. **Embracing E-Commerce:** Dell was an early adopter of e-commerce. The company's website became a crucial platform for sales and customer interaction, allowing customers to configure and purchase computers

online — a revolutionary concept in the 1990s.

4. Expansion and Diversification: Under Dell's leadership, the company expanded its product line beyond desktops to include laptops, servers, storage devices, and peripherals. This diversification strategy helped Dell capture a broader market and sustain growth.

5. Acquisitions and Innovations: Dell's approach to growth included strategic acquisitions, such as Perot Systems and EMC Corporation, to strengthen its capabilities in IT services and storage solutions. These acquisitions also facilitated Dell's transformation into a comprehensive technology solutions provider.

6. Focus on Customer Feedback: Throughout Dell's evolution, customer feedback played a crucial role. Dell implemented feedback loops to continuously improve products and customer service, demonstrating a commitment to meeting customer needs.

7. Philanthropic Initiatives: Beyond business success, Michael Dell has been active in philanthropy through the Michael & Susan Dell Foundation, focusing on education, healthcare, and family economic stability.

Michael Dell's entrepreneurial journey is characterised by creativity in business model innovation, strategic foresight in market expansion, and a strong focus on customer-centricity. His ability to adapt to technological advancements and market demands has solidified Dell Technologies as a prominent player in the global technology industry.

Creative Entrepreneurship of Jack Ma

Jack Ma, the co-founder of Alibaba Group, exemplifies creative entrepreneurship through several key aspects of his journey:

1. **Visionary Leadership:** Jack Ma's entrepreneurial journey began with a vision to connect Chinese manufacturers with global markets using the internet. This vision was ahead of its time in China during the late 1990s when internet penetration was low.

2. **Innovative Business Model:** Alibaba started as a business-to-business (B2B) online marketplace, Alibaba.com, catering to small and medium-sized enterprises (SMEs). This platform allowed SMEs in China to reach customers globally, democratising international trade.

3. **Adaptability and Diversification:** Over the years, Alibaba diversified its business model into various sectors including e-commerce (Taobao and Tmall), digital payments (Alipay), cloud computing (Alibaba Cloud), and more. This diversification helped Alibaba become one of the largest tech conglomerates globally.

4. **Social Responsibility:** Jack Ma has emphasised the importance of social responsibility and philanthropy. He initiated the Alibaba Foundation and donated generously towards education and environmental causes, showcasing a blend of business success and social impact.

5. **Global Expansion:** Under Jack Ma's leadership, Alibaba expanded its footprint globally, aiming to compete with global giants like Amazon and eBay. This expansion included investments in Southeast Asia, India, and other markets.

6. Championing Small Businesses: One of Jack Ma's core beliefs is empowering small businesses. Alibaba's platforms provide tools and resources for SMEs to thrive in the digital economy, enabling entrepreneurship on a massive scale in China and beyond.

7. Challenges and Resilience: Despite facing challenges, including regulatory hurdles and competition, Jack Ma's resilience and strategic foresight enabled Alibaba to navigate complexities and maintain its position as a leading tech innovator.

Jack Ma's journey as a creative entrepreneur is marked by his visionary leadership, innovative business models, global ambitions, social responsibility, and commitment to empowering small businesses. His impact extends beyond business success, influencing the global tech landscape and inspiring future generations of entrepreneurs.

Creative Entrepreneurship of Brian Chesky

Brian Chesky is best known as one of the co-founders and the CEO of Airbnb, a company that has revolutionised the travel and hospitality industry. His approach to entrepreneurship can be seen as highly creative and innovative, reshaping the way people think about accommodation and travel experiences.

Here are some key aspects of Brian Chesky's creative entrepreneurship:

1. Identifying an Unmet Need: Chesky and his co-founders identified a gap in the market for affordable, unique accommodation options that could provide a more personal experience than traditional hotels. This led to the concept of Airbnb, where people could rent out their homes or spare rooms to travellers.

2. **Building a Community:** Chesky understood the importance of creating a community around Airbnb. He focused on building trust and connection among hosts and guests through user reviews, profiles, and shared interests. This community aspect not only differentiated Airbnb but also helped in scaling the platform.

3. **Innovative Business Model:** Airbnb introduced a disruptive business model that challenged the established norms of the hospitality industry. By leveraging existing resources (people's homes) instead of building new infrastructure, Airbnb could rapidly expand its offerings globally at a minimal cost.

4. **Embracing Design Thinking:** Chesky, who has a background in design, brought a design-centric approach to Airbnb. He emphasised the importance of user experience, aesthetics, and functionality in every aspect of the platform, from website design to the booking process and beyond.

5. **Adapting to Challenges:** Over the years, Airbnb faced regulatory challenges, especially in cities with strict housing laws. Chesky demonstrated adaptability by working with regulators, refining policies, and finding ways to comply with local laws while continuing to grow the business.

6. **Diversification and Expansion:** Under Chesky's leadership, Airbnb expanded beyond just accommodation bookings to include experiences and adventures, catering to travellers seeking unique activities and local insights.

7. Crisis Management: During the COVID-19 pandemic, when travel ground to a halt, Chesky navigated Airbnb through a challenging period by focusing on long-term sustainability, trimming costs, and diversifying revenue streams.

Brian Chesky's approach to creative entrepreneurship involves a blend of vision, innovation, community-building, and adaptability. By challenging conventions and focusing on user needs, he has successfully transformed Airbnb into a global brand that continues to shape the future of travel and hospitality.

Creative Entrepreneurship of Garrett Camp

Garrett Camp is a fascinating figure in the realm of entrepreneurship, particularly known for co-founding Uber, a revolutionary ride-sharing platform. His journey as a creative entrepreneur spans beyond just Uber, showcasing a blend of innovation, vision, and business acumen.

Early Ventures and Entrepreneurial Spirit

Garrett Camp's entrepreneurial journey began early. Before Uber, he co-founded StumbleUpon in 2001, a pioneering web-discovery platform that allowed users to discover and recommend web content based on personal preferences. StumbleUpon gained significant popularity and was eventually acquired by eBay in 2007 for $75 million, marking a successful exit for Camp and his team.

The Birth of Uber

However, Garrett Camp's most well-known venture is Uber, which he co-founded in 2009 along with Travis Kalanick and others. Uber revolutionised the transportation industry by introducing a platform that seamlessly connected riders with drivers through a mobile app. This disruptive innovation not only transformed urban transportation but also laid the foundation for the gig economy globally.

Entrepreneurial Vision and Innovation

Camp's entrepreneurial style is characterised by a strong focus on solving real-world problems through technology and innovation. Uber's success can be attributed to Camp's vision of improving urban mobility, enhancing convenience for consumers, and creating economic opportunities for drivers.

Beyond Uber

Apart from Uber and StumbleUpon, Camp has also been involved in various other ventures and investments. He co-founded Expa, a startup studio that helps build and launch new companies, aiming to apply lessons learned from Uber and other successful ventures to new projects.

Impact and Legacy

Garrett Camp's impact on the entrepreneurial landscape extends beyond his individual ventures. His success with Uber has inspired countless entrepreneurs and startups to innovate and disrupt traditional industries using technology. His approach to entrepreneurship emphasises the importance of identifying market needs, leveraging technology, and creating scalable solutions.

Garrett Camp is not only a creative entrepreneur but also a visionary who has significantly influenced the tech industry with his innovative ventures. From StumbleUpon to Uber and beyond, Camp's journey underscores the power of entrepreneurship in driving societal change and creating value on a global scale. His story continues to inspire aspiring entrepreneurs to think big, take risks, and pursue their visions relentlessly.

Creative Entrepreneurship of Melanie Perkins

Melanie Perkins is a fascinating figure in the realm of creative entrepreneurship, best known for co-founding Canva, a popular graphic design platform. Her journey exemplifies several key aspects of successful entrepreneurship:

1. **Identifying a Pain Point:** Perkins recognised the complexity of graphic design software and saw an opportunity to simplify the process for non-designers.

2. **Vision and Innovation:** She envisioned a platform that would democratise design, making it accessible to everyone regardless of their skill level.

3. **Execution and Resilience:** Alongside her co-founders, Perkins started Canva despite initial rejections and challenges. Their perseverance eventually led to its widespread adoption.

4. **User-Centric Design:** Canva's success can be attributed to its intuitive interface and focus on user experience, which resonated with millions

worldwide.

5. Scaling and Global Impact: Under Perkins' leadership, Canva grew exponentially, attracting users and investors globally, thus revolutionising the graphic design landscape.

6. Community and Culture: Perkins fostered a culture of creativity and inclusivity within Canva, which helped in attracting top talent and retaining a loyal user base.

7. Philanthropy and Social Impact: Beyond business success, Perkins has been involved in philanthropic efforts, aiming to empower women in technology and education.

Melanie Perkins exemplifies how combining innovation, determination, and a deep understanding of user needs can lead to the creation of a globally influential and successful company like Canva. Her story serves as inspiration for aspiring entrepreneurs looking to make a significant impact in their respective industries.

Creative Entrepreneurship of Oprah Winfrey

Oprah Winfrey is a quintessential example of creative entrepreneurship, having built an empire that spans media, entertainment, and beyond. Here are some key aspects of Oprah's entrepreneurial journey:

1. Vision and Passion: Oprah's career began with a vision to connect with audiences through storytelling and meaningful conversations. She recognised the power of media to inspire and educate.

2. Innovation in Media: Oprah revolutionised daytime television with "The Oprah Winfrey Show," which became a platform for discussing important social issues, personal development, and promoting positive change.

3. Brand Building: Oprah effectively built a personal brand synonymous with authenticity, empathy, and empowerment. Her influence extended to various media ventures, including magazines, books, and production companies.

4. Diversification and Expansion: Beyond television, Oprah diversified her business interests. She founded Harpo Productions, launched the OWN network, and invested in diverse ventures, demonstrating her entrepreneurial acumen and business savvy.

5. Social Impact: Oprah's entrepreneurship is deeply intertwined with social impact. She has championed causes related to education, literacy, and empowerment, leveraging her platform and resources to effect positive change.

6. Adaptability and Resilience: Throughout her career, Oprah navigated challenges, setbacks, and industry shifts with resilience. Her ability to evolve and adapt to new media landscapes underscores her entrepreneurial spirit.

7. Philanthropy and Leadership: Oprah is committed to philanthropy, donating to various charitable causes and establishing the Oprah Winfrey Foundation to support education and empowerment initiatives.

Oprah Winfrey's entrepreneurial journey exemplifies how creativity, authenticity, and a commitment to making a difference can lead to tremendous success and influence. She continues to inspire millions globally as a role model for aspiring entrepreneurs and leaders in media and beyond.

Creative Entrepreneurship of Adam Neumann

Adam Neumann is known for co-founding WeWork, a company that initially gained rapid success and attention for its innovative approach to co-working spaces. His journey as a creative entrepreneur includes several key elements:

1. **Visionary Idea:** Neumann envisioned transforming traditional office spaces into vibrant, community-focused environments that foster collaboration and creativity. WeWork aimed to provide more than just workspace but also a lifestyle and community for freelancers, startups, and larger corporations.

2. **Disruptive Innovation:** WeWork disrupted the real estate industry by offering flexible lease agreements and transforming underutilised spaces into dynamic co-working hubs. This model appealed to entrepreneurs and businesses seeking flexibility and a sense of community.

3. **Scaling and Expansion:** Under Neumann's leadership, WeWork expanded rapidly, establishing a global presence with numerous locations across major cities worldwide. This growth was fuelled by significant investments and a strong brand presence.

4. **Brand and Culture:** Neumann cultivated a unique company culture at WeWork, emphasising community, collaboration, and innovation. This

culture contributed to the company's appeal among entrepreneurs and startups.

5. Challenges and Controversies: Despite initial success, WeWork faced challenges, including financial losses and scrutiny over its valuation and corporate governance practices. Neumann's management style and decisions came under criticism, leading to his eventual departure from the company.

6. Legacy and Lessons: Adam Neumann's entrepreneurial journey with WeWork highlights the importance of innovation, vision, and understanding market needs. It also underscores the risks associated with rapid expansion and the need for sustainable business practices.

7. Impact on Industry: Although WeWork faced setbacks, it left a lasting impact on the real estate and co-working industry, influencing how companies approach office space and community-building.

Adam Neumann's story serves as a cautionary tale in entrepreneurial circles, emphasising the balance between ambitious growth and sustainable business practices. His experience with WeWork illustrates both the potential and challenges of scaling a disruptive business model in a competitive market.

Creative Entrepreneurship of Rihanna

Rihanna, beyond her iconic status as a singer and performer, has also established herself as a creative entrepreneur through several ventures:

1. **Fenty Beauty:** Rihanna launched Fenty Beauty in 2017, aiming to address the lack of inclusivity in the beauty industry. The brand gained immediate acclaim for its extensive range of foundation shades that cater to diverse skin tones. This move not only filled a gap in the market but also set a new standard for inclusivity in beauty products.

2. **Savage X Fenty:** In 2018, Rihanna founded Savage X Fenty, a lingerie line known for its size-inclusive and diverse range of products. The brand emphasises body positivity and celebrates different shapes and sizes, challenging traditional beauty standards in the fashion industry.

3. **Fashion Ventures:** Rihanna's influence extends to the fashion world through collaborations with brands like Puma and her own luxury fashion line under LVMH, Fenty Maison. Her fashion ventures are known for pushing boundaries and reflecting her personal style, blending street-wear with high fashion.

4. **Music and Branding:** Throughout her music career, Rihanna has demonstrated a keen sense of branding and marketing. She has leveraged her image and influence to endorse products and collaborate with brands, further expanding her entrepreneurial footprint.

5. **Philanthropy and Social Impact:** Rihanna is actively involved in philanthropy and advocacy, particularly in education and healthcare in developing countries. Her Clara Lionel Foundation supports initiatives around the world, emphasising the importance of giving back and creating social change.

6. **Cultural Influence:** Rihanna's entrepreneurial endeavours are deeply connected to her cultural influence and ability to resonate with diverse audiences worldwide. Her ventures often reflect her values of inclusivity,

empowerment, and self-expression.

7. Business Acumen: Rihanna's success as a creative entrepreneur is underpinned by her strategic vision, understanding of market trends, and ability to capitalise on her influence to drive business growth and social impact.

Rihanna exemplifies creative entrepreneurship through her innovative ventures in beauty, fashion, and philanthropy. She has successfully disrupted industries, challenged norms, and empowered individuals through her diverse and inclusive brands. Her entrepreneurial journey continues to inspire both within and beyond the realms of music and entertainment.

AI AND CREATIVE ENTREPRENEURSHIP

Unleashing Creative Entrepreneurship

IN the dynamic landscape of contemporary business world, entrepreneurs are constantly seeking innovative ways to stay ahead. Therefore, the fusion of artificial intelligence (AI) and entrepreneurial creativity has emerged as a powerful catalyst for innovation and success. As we stand at the intersection of technology and commerce, the symbiotic relationship between AI and the art of business is reshaping the entrepreneurial landscape. This paradigm shift gives rise to a phenomenon that transcends traditional boundaries — unleashing creative entrepreneurship. The integration of Artificial Intelligence (AI) into the fabric of business operations has not only become a necessity but also a catalyst for creative entrepreneurship. This chapter delves into the profound impact of AI on the art of business, exploring how it can transform traditional models and empowers entrepreneurs to chart new territories.

This exploration delves into the multifaceted ways in which AI and the art of business converge to create a fertile ground for groundbreaking ideas, disruptive solutions, and unprecedented market ventures. From leveraging machine learning algorithms to unearth untapped market trends to utilising neural networks to enhance creative ideation, the possibilities are as boundless as the imagination itself.

The Synergy of Artificial Intelligence and the Art of Business

IN this era of rapid technological advancement, artificial intelligence stands as a game-changer, offering unprecedented opportunities for those who dare to explore the uncharted territories of business innovation. The intricate relationship between human creativity and the computational prowess of AI has given birth to a synergy that not only amplifies the scope of entrepreneurial endeavours but also redefines the very essence of what it means to be a business visionary.

We are on a journey where the lines between human ingenuity and artificial intelligence blur, forging a path towards a new era of entrepreneurship — one that embraces the transformative power of technology without sacrificing the essence of human creativity. As we navigate this intricate tapestry of innovation by unleashing creative entrepreneurship, the synergy of Artificial Intelligence and the art of business unveils the secrets, strategies, and success stories that illuminate the road ahead for those seeking to pioneer the next wave of business evolution. Aspiring entrepreneurs must have the mindset to embark on a quest that transcends the conventional, as we unlock the immense potential lying at the intersection of AI and the artful spirit of entrepreneurship.

Artificial Intelligence in the Business

Artificial Intelligence (AI) has become a transformative force in the business world, revolutionising the way businesses operate, make decisions, and engage with customers. The integration of AI technologies offers numerous advantages across various business functions, enhancing efficiency, productivity, and strategic decision-making. Here are key aspects of AI in the business landscape:

Automation and Efficiency

Business Processes: AI automates repetitive and time-consuming tasks, allowing employees to focus on more complex and creative aspects of their roles.

Cost Reduction: Automation through AI can significantly reduce operational costs by streamlining processes and minimising errors.

Data Analysis and Decision Making

Data Processing: AI systems can process vast amounts of data quickly and accurately, providing valuable insights into market trends, customer behaviour, and operational efficiency.

Predictive Analytics: AI algorithms can predict future trends and outcomes based on historical data, aiding in strategic decision-making and risk management.

Customer Experience Enhancement

Personalisation: AI enables businesses to provide personalised experiences to customers by analysing their preferences, behaviours, and purchasing patterns.

Chatbots and Virtual Assistants: AI-powered chatbots enhance customer support by providing instant responses to queries, improving customer satisfaction and reducing response times.

Supply Chain Optimisation

Demand Forecasting: AI helps businesses optimise their supply chain by predicting demand fluctuations, reducing excess inventory, and minimising stock-outs.

Logistics and Transportation: AI can improve route planning, reduce delivery times, and enhance overall logistics efficiency.

Cybersecurity

Threat Detection: AI plays a crucial role in identifying and mitigating cybersecurity threats by analysing patterns and anomalies in network traffic and system behaviour.

Fraud Prevention: AI algorithms can detect unusual patterns in financial transactions, helping prevent fraudulent activities.

Human Resources and Talent Management

Recruitment: AI tools can streamline the recruitment process by automating resume screening, identifying suitable candidates, and even conducting initial interviews.

Employee Engagement: AI-powered systems can analyse employee feedback, helping businesses improve workplace satisfaction and productivity.

Innovation and Product Development

Market Research: AI facilitates comprehensive market research by analysing online discussions, social media, and industry trends to identify opportunities and threats.

Design and Prototyping: AI algorithms can assist in product design and prototyping, accelerating the innovation process.

Compliance and Risk Management

Regulatory Compliance: AI can assist businesses in ensuring compliance with ever-changing regulations by automating monitoring and reporting processes.

Risk Assessment: AI tools help businesses assess and manage risks by analysing data and identifying potential issues.

Competitive Advantage

Strategic Insights: AI provides businesses with strategic insights and a competitive edge by processing and interpreting vast amounts of data, enabling informed decision-making.

In conclusion, the integration of AI in business operations is no longer a luxury but a necessity for staying competitive in today's dynamic market. As technology continues to evolve, businesses that leverage AI effectively will be better positioned to adapt to changing landscapes, innovate, and thrive in the digital era.

AI's Role in Creative Entrepreneurship

AI is not just a technological advancement; it's a paradigm shift that redefines the very essence of entrepreneurship. Gone are the days when success solely hinged on conventional strategies; today, creativity and adaptability are paramount. AI, with its ability to process vast amounts of data and generate insights, serves as a game-changer for entrepreneurs looking to make informed decisions and drive innovation.

The following case studies highlight the transformative impact of Artificial Intelligence on creative entrepreneurship across various sectors.

Case Study 1: Enhancing Customer Experiences with AI

Consider the case of a boutique e-commerce platform that leverages AI-powered recommendation engines. By analysing user behaviour and preferences, the platform tailors product recommendations, creating a personalised shopping experience. This not only boosts customer satisfaction but also increases sales and customer loyalty. The fusion of AI and the art of business transforms the mundane act of shopping into a personalised, engaging journey.

Breaking Barriers with Data-Driven Creativity: In the realm of creative entrepreneurship, data is the new currency. AI equips entrepreneurs with the ability to extract meaningful insights from vast datasets, facilitating informed decision-making. By understanding customer behaviour, market trends, and emerging patterns, entrepreneurs can identify opportunities and craft strategies that resonate with their target audience.

Case Study 2: Adaptive Marketing Strategies

A marketing agency harnesses the power of AI to analyse social media trends and consumer sentiments in real-time. This enables the agency to dynamically adjust marketing campaigns, ensuring they align with the ever-evolving preferences of their audience. The result is a marketing strategy that not only captures attention but also adapts to changing market dynamics, showcasing the synergy between AI and creative entrepreneurship.

AI as a Catalyst for Innovation: The essence of entrepreneurship lies in pushing boundaries and bringing fresh perspectives to the table. AI acts as a catalyst for innovation, providing entrepreneurs with tools to explore uncharted territories and redefine industries. From automated product design to predictive analytics, AI fosters a culture of innovation where creativity flourishes.

Case Study 3: Disrupting Traditional Industries

Consider an AI-driven startup entering the insurance sector. By leveraging machine learning algorithms, the startup streamlines the claims process, reducing turnaround times and enhancing accuracy. This disruption not only improves operational efficiency but also challenges established norms, illustrating how AI can fuel innovation and redefine the landscape of traditional industries.

AI-Driven Collaboration: Human and Machine Synergy

One of the most profound aspects of AI in creative entrepreneurship is its ability to enhance human capabilities. Rather than replacing human creativity, AI acts as a collaborative partner, augmenting our skills and enabling us to achieve feats previously deemed impossible.

Case Study 4: Collaborative Design in Architecture

In the field of architecture, AI assists designers by generating design alternatives based on specified parameters. Architects can then build upon these generated concepts, pushing the boundaries of their creativity. The result is a harmonious collaboration between human intuition and machine-generated possibilities, showcasing the symbiotic relationship between AI and creative entrepreneurship.

Ethical Considerations in the Age of AI: As entrepreneurs embrace the power of AI, it is crucial to address ethical considerations surrounding its use. Transparency, accountability, and responsible AI practices must be integral to the entrepreneurial journey. This not only safeguards against unintended consequences but also fosters a culture of trust among customers and stakeholders.

Case Study 5: Ethical AI in Healthcare

An AI-powered healthcare startup prioritises ethical considerations in its diagnostic algorithms. The algorithms not only provide accurate predictions but also offer transparency into the decision-making process, ensuring that healthcare professionals and patients can trust the technology. This commitment to ethics becomes a cornerstone of the startup's brand, showcasing the importance of responsible AI in creative entrepreneurship.

Pioneering the Future of Business: In the confluence of AI and the art of business, entrepreneurs find themselves at the forefront of a transformative era. The integration of AI is not merely a technological upgrade; it is a shift in mindset, a commitment to creativity, and a journey towards innovative excellence. As entrepreneurs harness the power of AI to navigate the complexities of the modern business landscape, they not only redefine their industries but also pave the way for a future where creative entrepreneurship thrives in harmony with artificial intelligence.

Case Study 6: Sustainable Supply Chain Optimisation

A forward-thinking fashion startup utilises AI to optimise its supply chain for sustainability. By analysing environmental data, consumer preferences, and production costs, the AI system recommends eco-friendly materials and efficient manufacturing processes. This not only reduces the ecological footprint of the business but also resonates with environmentally conscious consumers, showcasing how AI can drive both innovation and ethical business practices.

Case Study 7: Predictive Maintenance in Manufacturing

In the manufacturing sector, a company leverages AI for predictive maintenance of machinery. By analysing historical performance data and real-time sensor information, the AI system predicts potential equipment failures before they occur. This proactive approach minimises downtime, reduces maintenance costs, and ensures smooth operations. The fusion of AI with manufacturing exemplifies how creative entrepreneurship can optimise processes for efficiency and longevity.

Case Study 8: AI-Enhanced Creativity in Content Creation

A digital media agency embraces AI tools for content creation, enabling them to automate routine tasks and amplify their creative output. Natural Language Processing (NLP) algorithms assist in generating engaging headlines, while image recognition technology helps in selecting compelling visuals. The creative team can then focus on higher-order tasks, resulting in a more dynamic and prolific content creation process. This case study illustrates how AI empowers creative entrepreneurs to amplify their creative capabilities.

Case Study 9: Personalised Learning Platforms

An EdTech startup revolutionises the education sector by implementing AI-driven personalised learning platforms. By analysing students' learning patterns, strengths, and weaknesses, the platform tailors educational content to meet individual needs. This not only enhances the learning experience but also contributes to improved academic performance. The fusion of AI and education exemplifies how entrepreneurs can leverage technology to cater to diverse learning styles and preferences.

Case Study 10: AI-Powered Financial Advisory

A fintech startup disrupts the traditional financial advisory model by incorporating AI into its services. The AI algorithm analyses market trends, economic indicators, and individual financial goals to provide personalised investment advice. This democratisation of financial services makes sophisticated investment strategies accessible to a broader audience, showcasing how AI can transform industries and make them more inclusive.

Case Study 11: Virtual Try-On Experiences in Retail

An innovative retail brand integrates AI into its online platform to offer virtual try-on experiences. Using augmented reality and computer vision, customers can virtually try on clothing and accessories before making a purchase. This not only enhances the online shopping experience but also reduces the likelihood of returns, showcasing how AI can bridge the gap between the digital and physical retail worlds.

Case Study 12: AI-Driven Social Impact Initiatives

A social impact-focused startup employs AI to address pressing societal issues. By analysing demographic data, the startup identifies areas with specific needs and tailors its initiatives accordingly. Whether it's healthcare, education, or environmental conservation, the AI-driven approach allows for targeted and impactful interventions, showcasing how creative entrepreneurship can be a force for positive change with the assistance of AI. These diverse case studies underscore the versatility of AI in fostering creative entrepreneurship across various industries. Whether optimising supply chains, transforming content creation, or revolutionising education, the synergy between AI and the art of business opens up new frontiers for innovation and growth. As entrepreneurs continue to explore and embrace AI technologies, the landscape of creative entrepreneurship is destined to evolve, shaping a future where ingenuity knows no bounds.

Case Study 13: AI-Driven Healthcare Diagnostics

A medical diagnostics startup pioneers the use of AI to enhance disease detection. By analysing medical imaging data, the AI system assists radiologists in identifying subtle patterns indicative of early-stage diseases. This not only improves diagnostic accuracy but also expedites the detection process, potentially saving lives. The integration of AI in healthcare showcases how technology can be a powerful ally in the pursuit of better patient outcomes.

Case Study 14: Dynamic Pricing in E-Commerce

An e-commerce giant embraces AI for dynamic pricing strategies. By analysing real-time market conditions, competitor pricing, and consumer behaviour, the AI system adjusts product prices dynamically. This not only maximises revenue but also ensures that consumers receive fair and competitive pricing. The case illustrates how AI can optimise pricing strategies, adding a layer of agility to traditional business models.

Case Study 15: AI-Enhanced Virtual Events

In response to the evolving landscape of events, an event management startup incorporates AI to enhance virtual experiences. By analysing participant engagement data, the AI system recommends personalised content, networking opportunities, and agenda adjustments in real-time. This dynamic approach ensures that virtual events are not only informative but also tailored to individual preferences, demonstrating how AI can redefine the way we engage in the digital realm.

Case Study 16: AI-Generated Music Composition

A music production company leverages AI algorithms to assist composers in generating innovative musical compositions. By understanding musical patterns, preferences, and historical data, the AI system suggests creative elements that complement the composer's style. This collaboration between human creativity and AI showcases how technology can be a source of inspiration and exploration in artistic endeavours.

Case Study 17: AI-Optimised Logistics in Agriculture

Agriculture undergoes a technological revolution as a smart farming startup employs AI to optimise logistics. By analysing weather patterns, soil conditions, and crop data, the AI system recommends optimal planting times, irrigation schedules, and harvesting windows. This precision agriculture approach not only increases crop yields but also promotes sustainability by minimising resource usage.

Case Study 18: AI in Human Resources for Talent Acquisition

A forward-thinking HR consultancy adopts AI to streamline talent acquisition processes. By analysing resumes, online profiles, and candidate interactions, the AI system identifies potential matches that align with company culture and job requirements. This not only accelerates the recruitment process but also ensures a more diverse and inclusive talent pool, illustrating how AI can be a valuable ally in human-centric aspects of business.

Case Study 19: AI-Powered Personal Finance Assistant

A fintech startup develops an AI-powered personal finance assistant that goes beyond traditional budgeting apps. By analysing spending patterns, financial goals, and market trends, the AI assistant provides personalised financial advice, investment strategies, and even anticipates potential financial challenges. This holistic approach to personal finance showcases how AI can empower individuals to make informed financial decisions.

Case Study 20: AI-Driven Virtual Fashion Design

In the fashion industry, a design studio integrates AI into the creative process. By analysing fashion trends, consumer preferences, and historical design data, the AI system generates design concepts that inspire human designers. This collaboration between AI and human creativity leads to the creation of cutting-edge fashion collections, highlighting how technology can serve as a catalyst for innovation in the world of design.

These case studies further illustrate the versatility of AI in driving creative entrepreneurship and transforming traditional business models. From healthcare and agriculture to music and fashion, the integration of AI opens up new possibilities for innovation, efficiency, and customer-centric approaches. As entrepreneurs continue to explore the potential of AI, the boundaries of creative entrepreneurship will continue to expand, shaping a future where technology and human ingenuity coalesce for unprecedented success.

BONUS

Welcome to CyberVIEW!

As a bonus, I'm offering free, unlimited access to my YouTube channel, https://youtube.com/@Cyber-View.

Connect with me to transform your digital life. You won't be overwhelmed by the frequency of the videos, as there will be consistent uploads. You'll have ample time to understand, learn, and practice. My content is designed with people who have low vision in mind, and I believe this approach will be beneficial for everyone. Discover innovative techniques, cutting-edge tools, and practical insights to enhance your WordPress and AI experience.

Please share and subscribe to my YouTube channel, and don't forget to enable notifications on your mobile device so you never miss out on useful free information.

SUBSCRIBE - https://youtube.com/@Cyber-View

RESOURCES

Welcome to MY Resources Page!
https://ashfaaq.com/resources

I'm thrilled you're here! This is your go-to hub for cutting-edge AI tools and digital products designed to boost productivity and spark creativity. Whether you're a seasoned professional or just starting out, these carefully selected resources will help you reach your goals and unlock your full potential. From intuitive AI software that streamlines workflows to innovative solutions that inspire, you'll find everything you need to elevate your work and projects.

Please note that many of these links are affiliate links, meaning I may earn a small commission at no extra cost to you when you make a purchase. This helps me continue bringing you the best resources and updates. I only recommend products I use for my projects, and your support means the world to me. This will always add value to your projects as well. Keep checking this page for exciting new AI tools and digital products.

Explore, discover, and let your journey to greater productivity and creativity begin!

Here's to your success and innovation!

Warm regards,
ASHFAAQ A. Khan

Conclusion

Recap of Key Points

AS you reach the end of this book, it's essential to look back and recap some of the key points that you've learned so far as an entrepreneur in the creative industry. The art of business is a challenging task, but with the right mindset, tools, and knowledge, you can set yourself up for success.

First and foremost, you need to have a clear understanding of your vision. Your vision is the driving force behind your business, and it will help you make decisions that align with your goals. You should also have a solid understanding of your target audience and what they need. Your products or services should solve a problem or fulfil a need for your ideal customers.

Another important point to consider is the power of branding. Your brand is what sets you apart from your competitors, and it's what people will remember you by. Make sure your brand is consistent across all channels, and it speaks to your audience.

Innovation is also critical in the creative industry. You need to be constantly evolving and creating new products or services to stay ahead of the game. Don't be afraid to take risks and try new things. You never know what might be the next big thing.

Networking is also a crucial part of being an entrepreneur. Attend industry events, join groups, and connect with like-minded individuals. You never know who might be able to help you in the future.

Finally, always remember to take care of yourself. Running a business can be stressful, and it's important to take breaks and recharge. Make time for self-care, and don't forget to celebrate your successes along the way.

In conclusion, being an entrepreneur in the creative industry requires a unique set of skills and knowledge. By understanding your vision, target audience, branding, innovation, networking, and self-care, you can set yourself up for success. Keep learning, growing, and pushing yourself to be the best you can be.

Encouragement to Pursue Creative Entrepreneurship

If you have a passion for creativity and a desire to turn that passion into a business, then you are a creative entrepreneur. You are someone who understands that the world needs more than just products and services – it needs innovation, inspiration, and imagination. As a creative entrepreneur, you have a unique opportunity to share your vision with the world and make a positive impact on society.

But pursuing creative entrepreneurship is not always easy. It requires a lot of hard work, dedication, and commitment. You will face challenges and obstacles along the way, and there will be times when you feel like giving up. However, if you stay focused on your goals and keep pushing through the tough times, you will be rewarded with the satisfaction of seeing your dreams become a reality.

So, if you are considering pursuing creative entrepreneurship, here are some words of encouragement to help you get started:

1. **Believe in yourself:** You have a unique perspective and a valuable set of skills that can help you succeed as a creative entrepreneur. Trust in your abilities and have faith in your vision.

2. **Take risks:** Creative entrepreneurship is all about taking risks and trying new things. Don't be afraid to step outside of your comfort zone and explore new opportunities.

3. **Surround yourself with supportive people:** Building a successful business can be challenging, but having a supportive network of friends, family, and mentors can make all the difference.

4. **Stay true to your values:** As a creative entrepreneur, you have the power to shape your business in a way that aligns with your values and beliefs. Stay true to who you are and what you stand for.

5. **Embrace failure:** Failure is a natural part of the creative process. Don't be discouraged by setbacks – use them as opportunities to learn and grow.

6. **Stay curious:** Creative entrepreneurship is all about curiosity and

exploration. Stay open-minded and always be willing to learn and try new things.

In conclusion, pursuing creative entrepreneurship can be a challenging but rewarding journey. By believing in yourself, taking risks, surrounding yourself with supportive people, staying true to your values, embracing failure, and staying curious, you can create a successful business that reflects your unique vision and passion. So, go forth and pursue your dreams – the world is waiting for your creative ideas!

FINAL THOUGHTS

Congratulations, you have made it to the end of ***AI and The Art of Business: A Guide to Creative Entrepreneurship***. I hope that you have found this book to be an informative and valuable resource that has inspired and motivated you to pursue your dreams of becoming a successful creative entrepreneur.

Throughout this book, I have covered a wide range of topics and provided you with practical advice and strategies for starting and growing your creative business. From developing your business idea and creating a business plan, to marketing and managing your business, I have shared with you the knowledge and expertise that can help you achieve your goals. As a creative entrepreneur, you have a unique set of skills and talents that can help you stand out in a crowded marketplace. You have the ability to bring new ideas and innovations to the table, and to create products and services that resonate with your audience.

However, starting and growing a business can be challenging, and it requires a lot of hard work, dedication, and perseverance. There will be times when you will face obstacles and setbacks, but it is important to remember that these challenges are opportunities to learn and grow. As you move forward on your entrepreneurial journey, I encourage you to stay focused on your goals, stay true to your passions and values, and never be afraid to take risks and try new things. Surround yourself with a supportive network of mentors, advisors, and peers who can provide you with guidance and feedback, and who can help you stay motivated and accountable.

Remember that success is not just about making money or achieving fame and recognition. It is also about making a positive impact on the world, and using your talents and resources to improve the lives of others. As a creative entrepreneur, you have the power to create meaningful change, and to inspire others to do the same.

So, go out there and chase your dreams. Be bold, be creative, and be persistent. With hard work, determination, and a little bit of luck, you can achieve anything you set your mind to.

Good luck!

Epilogue

IN the inspiring aftermath of ***AI and The Art of Business: A Guide to Creative Entrepreneurship***, a symphony of success echoes through the entrepreneurial realm. The guide, a catalyst for innovation, sparks a revolution in thinking, urging dreamers to embrace the canvas of commerce with artistic fervour. The epilogue is a celebration of triumphs — a gallery showcasing startups that metamorphose into vibrant enterprises, and individuals who weave their narratives with threads of creativity and resilience. Readers, once novices, emerge as architects of their destinies, wielding the brush of imagination to paint their ventures into masterpieces. As the final words linger, a resounding encouragement resonates — the belief that unconventional ideas, coupled with strategic acumen, can defy norms and shape a prosperous future. ***AI and The Art of Business: A Guide to Creative Entrepreneurship*** is not merely a guide; it's a compass pointing towards a realm where entrepreneurship becomes a dance of passion and strategy.

May this epilogue be an anthem for those venturing into the entrepreneurial mosaic, a reminder that every stroke of creativity contributes to a larger masterpiece, and that the art of business is an ever-evolving symphony, inviting all to play their unique melodies with courage and conviction.

ENDNOTES

Artificial Intelligence (AI) and Its Future

Artificial Intelligence (AI) refers to the design of computer systems that can perform tasks traditionally requiring human intelligence—such as learning, reasoning, problem-solving, and adapting to new information. In the context of business and entrepreneurship, AI is more than just a tool; it's a creative force reshaping how ideas are developed, markets are understood, and innovations are brought to life.

As explored in ***AI and The Art of Business: A Guide to Creative Entrepreneurship***, the future of AI lies not only in automation and efficiency but in enabling more intuitive, imaginative, and personalised approaches to building value. From data-driven insights to generative creativity, AI empowers entrepreneurs to push boundaries—redefining industries, customer experiences, and even the role of the entrepreneur.

Yet, with this power comes responsibility. The ethical, social, and strategic implications of AI will increasingly shape the entrepreneurial landscape. Its future depends on how wisely we harness its potential—balancing innovation with intention, and technology with humanity. AI raises urgent ethical questions about bias, autonomy, privacy, and the very nature of intelligence. As AI continues to evolve, its future will be defined not only by technological advances but by the choices humanity makes about how to guide, govern, and integrate it into society.

The Future of Business and the Role of the Entrepreneurs

As we navigate an era defined by rapid technological change, global interconnectedness, and shifting societal values, entrepreneurship emerges not just as a path to personal success, but as a critical force driving innovation, sustainability, and inclusive growth. Entrepreneurship today goes far beyond launching a startup or turning a profit. It is about solving real-world problems, identifying untapped opportunities, and building innovative, sustainable solutions.

The future of business will be shaped by those who are willing to take risks, embrace continuous learning, and rethink traditional models. It will require a mindset that blends creativity with resilience, and ambition with responsibility. Whether through tech-driven disruption, social innovation, or community-centered enterprises, entrepreneurs are uniquely positioned to drive meaningful change.

The future of business will not be built solely by large institutions, but by individuals and small teams willing to challenge convention, embrace uncertainty, and create value with purpose. In an uncertain world, one thing remains constant: the future belongs to those bold enough to create it.

Entrepreneurship is no longer confined to profit; it is about impact. And in that vision, the next chapter of business belongs to those who dare to build what doesn't yet exist.

The Role of Creativity in Entrepreneurial Success

Creativity plays a foundational role in entrepreneurship, shaping how entrepreneurs recognise opportunities, solve problems, and navigate uncertainty. It is not merely the spark for innovation but the engine that drives differentiation and long-term sustainability. Early economic theorist Joseph Schumpeter (1934) described the entrepreneur as a disruptor—someone who brings about "creative destruction" by replacing old industries or methods with more efficient ones, underscoring creativity as a critical function of entrepreneurial activity.

Modern entrepreneurship literature expands on this view, emphasising creativity as both a cognitive and behavioural skill. Research shows that individuals with high creative self-efficacy are more likely to pursue entrepreneurial ventures, adapt to changing market conditions, and persist through failure (Tierney & Farmer, 2002; Fillis & Rentschler, 2010). Creativity allows entrepreneurs to reframe constraints as opportunities, whether through resourcefulness in the face of limited capital or novel approaches to customer engagement.

In practice, creativity manifests across all stages of entrepreneurial development—from the initial idea generation and business modelling to branding, marketing, product design, and team-building. Particularly in the digital age, where disruption is constant and innovation cycles are shorter, the ability to think creatively is more vital than ever. As such, cultivating creativity should be viewed as a strategic priority for entrepreneurs and those who support them through education, policy, and investment.

A Note from the Author

Reflection:

1. **The Intersection of Code and Creativity**: Writing this book reinforced a powerful truth: creativity and technology are not opposites—they're allies. AI is not just a tool for automation; it's a collaborator in innovation, capable of amplifying human imagination in business.
2. **Entrepreneurship in the Age of Intelligence**: Today's entrepreneur must be part artist, part strategist, and part technologist. The real opportunity lies not just in using AI, but in learning how to think with it—creatively, ethically, and boldly.
3. **Limitations and Responsibility**: AI is not a magic solution. Its use in business must be grounded in responsibility, transparency, and respect for human values. This book only scratches the surface of those conversations, but I hope it encourages deeper inquiry.
4. **Living Guide for a Moving Target**: The ideas here are not meant to be final. AI evolves. Markets shift. Creativity takes new forms. I hope this book serves as a flexible framework—something you can revisit, revise, and reimagine as your journey unfolds.
5. **The Future Is Collaborative**: Whether you're a solo creator or building a global company, the future of business will be shaped by collaboration—between humans, between machines, and between ideas. May this book be a companion in building something that matters.

The future belongs to those who merge creativity with courage—so step forward, harness the power of AI, trust your vision, and start building the business only you can create.